JOE EGG

Also by Peter Nichols
Published by Grove Press

The National Health

JOE EGG

by

Peter Nichols

Consulting editor: Henry Popkin

GROVE PRESS
New York

Published by Grove Press
a division of Wheatland Corporation
841 Broadway
New York, N.Y. 10003

ISBN: 0-8021-5115-9
Library of Congress Catalog Card Number: 68-21264

Manufactured in the United States of America

Distributed by Random House, Inc., New York

This book is printed on acid-free paper.

First Evergreen Edition 1978
16   15   14   13

Joe Egg was first performed as *A Day in the Death of Joe Egg* at the Citizens' Theatre, Glasgow, on May 9, 1967. The play was directed by Michael Blakemore, and the cast was as follows:

BRI	Joe Melia
SHEILA	Zena Walker
JOE	Barbara Goldman
PAM	Carole Boyer
FREDDIE	Michael Murray
GRACE	Joan Hickson

The American première was given on February 1, 1968, at the Brooks Atkinson Theater, New York, produced by Joseph Cates and Henry Fownes in association with Michael Medwin (for Memorial Ltd). The cast was as follows:

BRI	Albert Finney
SHEILA	Zena Walker
JOE	Susan Alpern
PAM	Elizabeth Hubbard
FREDDIE	John Carson
GRACE	Joan Hickson

Designed by ROBIN PIDCOCK

Music by ANDY PARK

Lighting and set supervision by LLOYD BURLINGAME

CHARACTERS

BRI

SHEILA

JOE

PAM

FREDDIE

GRACE

JOE EGG

ACT ONE

BRI *and* SHEILA.

    BRI *comes on without warning. Shouts at audience.*

[handwritten note: ironic b/c from very beginning we're told that he's had enough, he can't stand it anymore.]

BRI : That's enough! (*Pause. Almost at once, louder.*) *I said enough!*
(*Pause. Stares at audience. He is thirty-three but looks younger.
Hardly ever at rest, acts being maladroit but the act is skilful.
Clowning may give way to ineffectual hectoring and then self-
piteous gloom.*)
Another word and you'll all be here till five o'clock. Nothing
to me, is it? I've got all the time in the world. (*Moves across
without taking his eyes off them.*) I didn't even get to the end
of the corridor before there was such a din all the other
teachers started opening their doors as much as to say what
the hell's going on there's SOMEBODY'S TALKING NOW! (*Pause,
stares again, like someone facing a mad dog.*) Who was it? You?
You, Mister Man? . . . I did not *accuse* you, I *asked* you.
Someone in the back row? (*Stares dumbly for some seconds.
Relaxes, moves a few steps. Shrugs.*) You're the losers, not
me. Who's that? (*Turns on them again.*) Right—hands on
heads! Come on, that includes you, put the comb away. Eyes
front and sit up. All of you, sit up! (*Puts his own hands on his
head for a while, watching for a move, waiting for a sound, then
takes them down. Suddenly roars.*) Hands on head and eyes
front! YOU I'm talking to! You'll be *tired* by the time I've
finished. Stand on your seat. And keep your hands on your
heads. Never mind what's going on outside, that joker at the
back. Keep looking out here. Eyes front, hands on heads.
(*Moves across.*)
(*Bell rings.*)
Who said MOVE? Nobody. Said move. Hands on heads . . .
Next one to groan stands on the seat. We're going to have
one minute's perfect silence before you go. (*Looks at his
watch.*) If we have to wait till midnight. (*Stands watching for*

some seconds.) That's nice. I like that. Now try to hold it just like that till I get to this machine-gun over here. (*Moves upstage, turning his back. Turns back at once.*) My fault, all right. Little joke. No more laughing. Eyes front, hands on heads. (*Waits for silence, looks at watch, moving across suddenly looks up, very cross again.*) Who was that? Whoever did—that—can open the window before we all get gassed . . . Wait a minute! Three of you? What are you—a group? One go—one nearest the window. All the others, eyes front, hands on heads. Right. (*Looks at watch.*) That characteristic performance from our friend near the window means we return to Go. (*Looks up sharply.*) Shall I make it *two* minutes? (*Looks down again. Ten seconds pass.*) We could have had this sooner. Then we shouldn't be wasting time sitting here when we might be . . . well . . . let's all—think—what we might be doing—'stead of sitting here when the rest have all gone home—we could be . . .

(*Speaking quietly now, absently staring into space. Few more seconds pass. When he speaks again, it is as if in a reverie.*) Yes—eyes front . . . hands on breasts . . . STOP the laughter! WHO wants to start another minute? (*Looks at watch then up again.*) And whatever the great joke is, whatever it is that has so tickled your Stone Age sense of humour—when all my efforts have failed . . . save it till you're outside. I'm going to get my coat from the staff-room now. And you will be as quiet as mice—no, fish—till I get back. All right? I don't want to hear a sound. Not a bubble. (*Goes off.*)

(*Lights up on set behind; Living-room.*)

(*Pleasant and comfortable, furnished with a gallant collection of junk-shop bargains and H.P. modern. Plain walls with two essential doors and one optional window. Door in upstage wall leads to hall and stairs, which can be seen when the door is opened. Door in other wall leads to kitchen. Bird in cage, fish in tank, plants in pots. Two paintings of cowboys are conspicuous.*)

(SHEILA, *wearing trousers and pullover, comes from kitchen with tea on a tray. She is thirty-five, generously built, serious and industrious. When dressed for society, she can be*

10

captivating. Puts down tray and runs back to kitchen door,
pushing with her foot, keeping out an animal.)
SHEILA: Back, back, no no.
　　(*Shuts the door and comes back. Door slams off.* SHEILA *starts*
　　pouring tea.)
　　(*Shouts.*) Bri?
BRI (*off*): No.
SHEILA (*shouts*): Just got tea.
　　(*He comes on, approaches her, takes the offered kiss, then*
　　stands close looking at her. She goes back to pouring tea and
　　offers him his cup. He doesn't take it, so she looks at his face.
　　She screams, nearly spills tea.)
　　What's that?
BRI: What?
SHEILA: On your face!
BRI: Where?
SHEILA: Near your eye.
BRI: What is it?
SHEILA: A black thing.
BRI: For Christ's sake——
SHEILA: A spider——
BRI: Shall I touch it?
SHEILA: A great black—get it off!
BRI: How?
SHEILA: Knock it off!
　　(BRI *takes it off, smiling.)*
SHEILA: Ugh!
　　(*He puts it on the back of his hand and shows her.)*
BRI: I confiscated it.
　　(*She knocks it away angrily.)*
　　From Terry Hughes.
SHEILA: Vicious sod!
BRI: He *is*. For thirteen.
SHEILA: You, I mean.
BRI: In Religious Instruction.
SHEILA: It's not funny.
BRI: What I told *him*.
　　(*She has turned from him. He sees he has done wrong and*

11

now tries to make amends. Approaches from behind and kisses her neck.)

SHEILA: Get away!

BRI: Oh, look——

SHEILA: Why d'you do it, Brian, honestly? You know that would upset me and the first thing you do——

BRI: Sorry, love.

SHEILA: I even kissed you——

BRI: Sorry.

(*He takes and drinks the tea. So does she. He puts down cup and kisses her again. Then caresses her.*)

Oh, love, if you knew how I'd been thinking of you——

SHEILA: You'll spill this tea.

BRI: Let's go to bed, come on.

SHEILA: Ow!—don't——

BRI: What?

SHEILA: Your hands are cold, you've just come in——

BRI: Let's go to bed.

SHEILA: At quarter to five?

BRI: I came home early specially.

SHEILA: The usual time.

BRI: Yeah, but I was *going* to keep them in.

SHEILA: Who?

BRI: Four D.

SHEILA: Did you *say* you would?

BRI: Yes.

SHEILA: To them?

BRI: Yes.

SHEILA: Then why didn't you?

BRI: I kept imagining our bed, our room, your legs thrashing about——

SHEILA: When *are* you going to learn?

BRI: My tongue half-way down your throat——
(*He is at her again.*)

SHEILA: You must carry out your threats.

BRI: —train screaming into tunnel——

SHEILA: They'll never listen to you if you don't——

BRI: —waves breaking on rocky shore.

12

(*She moves out of his reach. Pause. He sips tea, winces.*)
Sugar. (*He helps himself.*)

SHEILA: You want bromide.

BRI: I want you. It's you I want.
(*Turns, makes a joke of it, pointing to her like the advert.*)
I want you. Kitchener, look. I want you.
(*She smiles. He sits and drinks.*)

SHEILA: You should have kept them in.

BRI: I did for a bit. Then I left them with their hands on heads and went to fetch my coat and suddenly couldn't face them any more, so I never went back. Wonder how long they sat there.

SHEILA: Brian——

BRI: Terry Hodges, Fatty Brent . . . Glazebrook, the shop-steward—he's got a new watch. And of course Scanlon——
(*Shakes his head at the idea.*)
—the Missing Link. Pithecanthropus Erectus. *from the musical "On the Town" by Leonard Bernstein*

SHEILA: Has he flashed it lately?

BRI: Not at the teachers anyway.

SHEILA: Only that once.

BRI: That once was the only time it was reported.

SHEILA: Poor girl.

BRI: Some of the older women might keep quiet. Hope for more.

SHEILA: What happened to that girl?

BRI: Never heard of since.

SHEILA: Not surprising.

BRI: Shortest teaching career on record. Thirty-five minutes.
(*They drink.*)
No, I don't hate Scanlon any more. That's all a thing of the past. I just stare at him and wonder—is he only a monster of my own imagining? (*Mad Doctor voice comes on, not for the last time.*) 'Certainly, Nurse, he strangled a little girl, but that only means he's lonely. We must make him a mate.
(SHEILA *smiles. He drinks again.*)
No, you take this morning. I was on playground duty sipping my Nescaff, dreaming of a sudden painless road accident that would put an end to it all. Suddenly aware of the silence —too quiet for comfort. Few of the wilder elements sniggering

13

and casting crafty glances. Whipped round in time to spot
Scanlon sidling into the girls' bog. Went to the door and
shouted, "That boy, out of it!" Saw this figure zipping up his
flies in a panic. Not Scanlon at all.

SHEILA: No!

BRI: No. This new supply teacher.

SHEILA: Oh, no.

BRI: Yes.

SHEILA: Funny that way?

BRI: Not a bit. He didn't know it was the girls'. Only *looks*
about twelve even from the front. Dresses like them too.
Why can't he wear the right bloody uniform—tweedy
jacket and leather elbows—so we'd know whose side he's
on?

(*Pause again. He eats a biscuit.*)

SHEILA: Never mind. You break up in two days.

BRI: I broke up years ago.

(*Puts down cup. He embraces her. She disengages. He looks
at his hands.*)

BRI: Shall I put my gloves on?

SHEILA: What's the point of starting *now*? Joe's home any
minute.

BRI: Well?

SHEILA: Well! She's got to be fed, bathed, exercised, put to bed.
You know that.

(*Pause.*)

BRI: She can wait.

SHEILA: What?

BRI: Well, can't she?

SHEILA: Why should she? (*Pause.*) Anyway my rehearsal's at
seven and I promised to paint some scenery before that.

(BRI *moves away, kicks off shoes, sprawls in armchair. She
gives him more tea.*)

I shouldn't be late but your dinner's in the oven. On
automatic.

(*He takes out cigarette, finds matchbox is empty.*)

Take it out any time after seven. You'd never believe the
job I had finding a miniature bottle of Kirsch. In the local

14

off-licence they offered Spanish Van Rose instead. Luckily I was going into town so I got it there. I had to take those old clothes into the Unmarried Mothers. They were only collecting moths. What are you looking for?

BRI: Matches.

(*She gives them to him.*)

Collecting moths? The Unmarried Mothers?

SHEILA: The clothes. So I got the Kirsch at the same time. Oh, and all the wild-life's fed—the cats, the guinea-pigs, the goldfish, the stick-insects——

(*Pause.*)

BRI: The ginger-beer plant?

SHEILA: All the plants. Oh, remember not to let the cats in. I found a flea in here today again. And this afternoon I did my Oxfam collection and looked after Jenny's children while she got her coil fitted. (*Pause.*) Quite a day, one way or another. What are you thinking?

BRI: Wondering if we could have our guinea-pig fitted with a coil. Or guinea-sow, should it be? (*Scratches. Jumps out of the chair.*) I've got one now. (*Looks closely at chair for fleas.*)

SHEILA: If you've had a bad day, why don't you come with me?

BRI: Bad day? You ought to see the staffroom. Christmas Spirit nearly at breaking-point. Excuse me, I was under the impression that was my soap you're using—sod off!—I beg your pardon?—Sod off, matey—come outside and say that —grow up—no, I insist—come on—I sang: Great tidings of comfort and joy. But it fell on stony ground.

(*He sits on sofa, she sits beside him, takes his hand.*)

I said to my class, "Right—Christmas decorations—paper-chains." Deep voice from the back said, "Kids' stuff." I frowned at him and realized I'd never seen him before. Turned out he was the elder brother of one of the more backward boys. On the dole, he'd come in out of the cold, been sitting in classes all day, nobody'd noticed.

SHEILA: Did you throw him out?

BRI: What for? (*Smiles at recollection.*) When he brought me up his paper-chain, he said, "You're not much good at teaching, are you, mate?"

15

[handwritten margin note:] He's not committed to teaching. He doesn't even know who is in his class

[handwritten note below:] Represents his failure at teaching, at everything. He has no grasp or link with anything (except Sheila)

[handwritten note at bottom:] Sheila is Bri's only link to humanity, to reality, to life; that's why he holds onto her so childishly.

SHEILA. Oh, I should have hit him.

BRI: He meant it nicely. (*Smokes.*) I must find something else.

SHEILA: Come with me to rehearsal. Do you good to get out, see some pople.

BRI: What people? Freddie?

SHEILA: Plenty of whisky afterwards.

BRI: I should want the whisky first——

SHEILA: All right, first——

BRI: —if I had to talk to Freddie.

SHEILA: All right.

BRI: If I had to watch you caper about with muck on your face.

SHEILA: Shall I ring your mother and see if she's free?

BRI: Bloody hell! What a swinging prospect! My mother, Freddie——

SHEILA: I seem to remember——

BRI: And all that Kirsch bubbling away down there.

SHEILA: I seem to remember it was *you* introduced me to Freddie in the first place.

(*Doorbell rings.*)

BRI: There's Joe.

SHEILA: Remember that.

(BRI *gets up and makes for door while* SHEILA *shouts.*)
And at least I don't just sit about coining epigrams— wallowing in self-pity! At least I *do* something about it!

BRI: You and Freddie together, yes——

(*Goes off.*)

SHEILA (*shouts*): At least I try to make life work instead of——
(*Breaks off. Sighs deeply, almost as though doing an exercise in relaxation.*)
Honestly. (*Puts cups on tray and takes it off to kitchen.*)
Get away from the door then you won't get stepped on.
(*Shuts it behind her.*)
(*Pause.*)
(BRI *has left hall door open, showing hall and lower part of the stairs. He now comes back wheeling* JOE *in her invalid chair.*)
(JOE *is ten, physically normal but for the stiffness of her legs and arms. Her legs, at this stage, are covered with a blanket. She cannot support herself properly and has to be propped wherever*

16

she is put: for the most part, she lies supine. In her chair, she sits with the upper part of her body forward on the tray in front of her chair, as though asleep. Her face is pretty but vacant of expression, her voice feeble.)

(BRI *pushes her to the centre of the stage. He carries a small grip marked BOAC.*)

BRI: There we are then, lovely. Home again. (*Leaves her, puts down grip, looks at her.*) Safe and sound. You been a good girl?

JOE: A-aaah!

(*This is her closest approach to speech.*)

BRI: Really good?

JOE: Aaaah!

BRI: The lady in the bus said you'd been good. Sat by the driver, did you?

JOE: Aaaah!

BRI: There's a clever girl!

JOE: Aaaah!

BRI (*as though he understood*): Saw the Christmas trees?

JOE: Aaaah!

BRI: And the shops lit up?

JOE: Aaaah!

BRI: What d'you say? Saw *Jesus*? Where was he, where was Jesus, you poor softy?

(SHEILA *comes back.*)

JOE: Aaaah!

BRI: I see.

SHEILA: My great big beautiful darling home at last? (*Kneels by her chair.*) Got a great big beautiful kiss for Mummy? (*Kisses her.*)

JOE: Aaaah!

SHEILA: I'm lovely, she says.

BRI: Mad, she says, but lovely.

SHEILA: She been a good girl, Dad? Did the lady say?

BRI: Very good, Mum. She sat by the driver.

SHEILA (*mock amazement*): Did you sit by the driver? Did you, lovely?

(*They act as parents do receiving home a child of two from the*

17

Infants' School.)

BRI: Saw the Christmas trees, Mum.

SHEILA: Did you see the Christmas trees? *What* a clever girl!

BRI: And Jesus.

SHEILA: Jesus?

BRI: Bathed in light, in the sky.

SHEILA (*aside, to* BRI): She got a screw loose, Dad?

BRI: No, Mum.

SHEILA: Seeing Jesus?

BRI: On top the Electricity building.

SHEILA (*relieved*): Oh, yes! Thought she was off her chump for a minute, Dad.

BRI: Seeing Jesus in a dump like this? No wonder, Mum. But no, she's doing well, they say.

SHEILA: Daddy's pleased you're trying, love. What with your eleven-plus on the way.

(BRI *gives a short burst of laughter then resumes.*)

BRI: You want to get to a decent school.

SHEILA: I don't want to be shunted into some secondary modern slum, she says——

(*Kisses her again.*)

BRI: Like the one where Daddy works——

SHEILA: Share a room with forty or fifty council-house types and blackies.

BRI: No, I've had enough of them, she says, at the Spastics' Nursery. You want to go on to the Training Centre, help to make those ball-point pens.

(*Rummages in grip.*)

JOE: Aaaah!

SHEILA: I'm trying my hardest, she says.

BRI: You keep it up, my girl. Here's a note from Mrs.——

SHEILA: From the Nursery?

BRI: A school report, Mum. (*Reads.*) "Thank you for the present for Colin's birthday." Which is Colin?

SHEILA: Little boy who had meningitis.

BRI: Never stops whimpering?

SHEILA: That's him.

BRI: Did you send him Many Happy Returns?

18

SHEILA: I sent a card. And a cuddly bunny.

BRI: It's the thought that counts. (*Reads.*) "Quite a few of the parents remembered and the kitchen ladies made a lovely cake with seven candles and we held up Colin so he could see them burning, then we all helped him blow them out." (*Without looking at each other, they make the "Aaah" sound of a cinema audience being shown a new-born lamb.*) "The physiotherapist lady came and looked at us all today and said Josephine's shoulders show signs of improvement. She says keep on with the exercises."

SHEILA: Do your homework like a good girl. Daddy help.

BRI (*to* JOE): *She* won't be able to help. She's going out for a bit on the side.

SHEILA: Let me call your mother. Please.

BRI (*ignoring her, reading on*): Hullo, hullo, what's *this* I see? What's this? "She's had a few fits today but I think it must have been the excitement over Colin's cake." (*Moves about, acting cross father.* SHEILA *stops the comedy and begins to be seriously concerned.*)

SHEILA: Oh, dear, now why's that, I wonder?

BRI: Just you listen to me, my girl——

SHEILA: I thought we'd got them under control.

BRI: How are you to raise yourself above the general level if you keep having fits?

SHEILA: This is the first for weeks—except an occasional *petit mal.*

BRI: Those council-house types down there, what d'you think they say? (*Goes into a heavy village rustic act.*) "She puts it on, a voice you could cut with a knife—Lady Bleedin' Muck and no mistake! But look at her, she's no better than the likes of us, just another raver."

SHEILA: Poor kid, poor blossom.
(*Caresses* JOE.)

BRI: Spare the rod spoil the child, Mum.

SHEILA: I don't know why they've started.

BRI: Welfare State. Life's all too easy these days—free milk, show-jumping. Physiotherapy. Singing and candles. What singing and candles did we have at her age? Air-raids and clothing coupons and if we didn't like that, my mother used to say, "That be all you're getting, my sonner."

SHEILA: Hullo.

(JOE's *head has turned suddenly from right to left. Her body tenses. They watch silently.* JOE *remains staring towards her left. The right arm now stretches out as though commanding attention, the mouth begins to open and shut spasmodically, the eyes close, the head slowly and tensely returns from left to right. The legs are pulled up in the seizure. The opening and shutting of the mouth causes a distinct and explosive sucking sound.*)

(SHEILA *takes the note from* BRI's *hand and reads it.*)

That's great, that is. Explains it.

BRI: What?

SHEILA: They've run out of anti-convulsant suspension again.

BRI: Again?

SHEILA (*reading*): ". . . excitement over Colin's cake. Or perhaps because we've used up all her yellow medicine."

BRI: Call themselves a day nursery.

SHEILA: How many times is this?

BRI: Why don't they keep a few spare bottles in the 'fridge? Nearly all the kids need it.

SHEILA: The amount they use, they should have it on draught.

(*She goes to kitchen.* JOE's *fit has now finished. She rests on the shelf.* BRI *is excited by* SHEILA's *suggestion.*)

BRI: Yes! Drawn to the nurseries and day-centres in barrels by a dirty great fleet of dray-horses. (*Acts commentator with awe-struck voice. Holds hand-mike.*) And here—in the City Pharmacy—you can stand—as I'm standing now—in the nerve-centre of this great operation of mercy—and watch the myriad craftsmen at their various chores.

(SHEILA *comes back with two bottles and a spoon. They kneel, one each side of* JOE.)

SHEILA: Give her the phenos.

BRI: Or something less trad?

(*She hands him a bottle, which he opens and from which he pours two pills. She shakes the other bottle.*)

Bit more in keeping with our forward-looking technological society? A central pumping station and a vast complex of

20

underground culverts and sluice-gates.

SHEILA (*to* JOE): Soon be better, my flower.

(BRI *forces* JOE's *jaws apart and puts the pills into her mouth.*)

BRI: No, but they'll never stand for it.

SHEILA: Who?

BRI: Bristol's ratepayers. Cost a fortune.

SHEILA: Here, my blossom, lovely orange.

(*She spoons it in, with* BRI's *help.*)

BRI: Too fond of the ceremonial, the bullshit.

SHEILA: There's a clever girl.

(BRI *holds her jaw shut.*)

BRI: New life to dying crafts. Horse-brasses in the sun, tang of cooper's apron—(*Makes sound effects of horse-hooves, whinnying.*) Dagenham Girl Pipers.

(SHEILA *stoppers the bottles. Kisses* JOE.)

SHEILA: And for a special treat, Mummy got her favourite ice-cream for tea.

(BRI *releases her jaws.*)

BRI: Come down now.

SHEILA: Tell Mummy—are you wet?

(BRI *looks in the grip again. She puts her hand under* JOE's *blanket.*)

SHEILA: Soaking.

BRI: This nappy's dry.

SHEILA (*indignant*): Honestly! They've started *doing* that again this week. Leaving the one I send in the bag and letting her sit like Joe Egg in the damp all day. Her parts get spreathed.

BRI: Perhaps she *was dry* before the fit.

SHEILA: She could hardly have gone all day without a wee.

BRI: No.

SHEILA (*looks at watch*): Will *you* change her? I must go and get ready.

(BRI *throws nappy on* JOE's *chair-shelf, takes bottles from* SHEILA.)

If she's spreathed, there's ointment in the cupboard.

(*He nods, with a cheesy smile.*)

And if I were you, I should put her on the kitchen floor to change her.

21

BRI: I'm not the new nannie.
(*Pause.*)
SHEILA: No. 'Course not but——
BRI: I've done it before. Once or twice. In the last ten years.
(*He wheels* JOE *towards kitchen.*)
SHEILA: Brian.
(*He turns.*)
Shall I call your mother?
BRI: What for?
SHEILA: So we can go out.
BRI: Tuesday night there's nowhere much to go. The zoo's shut.
There's a Western at the Gaumont.
SHEILA: Come and see the rehearsal. Get drunk if you like. But
not too drunk to bring me home and have me.
BRI (*pointing to* JOE): *Pas devant*——
SHEILA: What?
BRI: *Pas devant l'enfant.*
SHEILA: Aitch-ay-vee-ee me.
(*She comes forward. He leaves chair and meets her. She
embraces him.*)
Seriously. Shall I?
(*He kisses her, buries his face in her hair, then emerges.*)
BRI: Hey, listen! What's it like with Freddie?
(*She stiffens, then struggles to break away but he holds her.*)
No, come on, you've told me about the others. Not all, of
of course——
SHEILA: Let go——
BRI: But a sampling—a cross-section——
SHEILA: I shall bite.
BRI: The ones that because of some exceptional feature stand out
from the crowd.
SHEILA: They were all before I met you.
BRI: But Freddie's *now*.
SHEILA: Let go.
BRI: What's his speciality?
SHEILA: Even if he wanted to—which he doesn't——
BRI: You must think I'm soft——
SHEILA: —Freddie would run a mile from a breath of scandal, you

22

know that!

BRI: No, but I mean—what's his gimmick?

SHEILA: Come and ask him——

BRI: For instance——

SHEILA: Why don't you?

BRI: —all your four Americans, you said, made you——

SHEILA: What? Where d'you get that?

BRI: What?

SHEILA: Four Americans.

BRI: Wrong?

SHEILA: Two Americans.

BRI: Oh.

SHEILA: One Canadian.

BRI: Ah. (*Releases her.*) Well. They made you lie across a pillow. I think they got it out of Hemingway. Then the Welshman —the stoker——

SHEILA: He wasn't a stoker. He was a policeman.

BRI: Oh, yes. He was shocked because you used bad words in a posh accent. But when it came to getting off your frock, he was so ravenous he tore it.

SHEILA: I wish I'd never told you anything. You said we should be *honest.* You told me all about yours first.

BRI (*nods*): All three. That took an hour. Then for the next few weeks you made a short-list.

SHEILA: You *made* me.

(*Pause.*)

JOE: A-aaah!

BRI: You must have enjoyed those fellows at the time.

SHEILA: No!

BRI: One or two.

SHEILA: I've told you.

BRI: Why go on with it then?

SHEILA: Once you get to a certain stage with a man, it's hard to say no.

BRI: Most women manage it. With *me*, at any rate. *Three* out of God knows how many tens of thousands I tried . . .

SHEILA: They didn't know a good thing when they saw it. You were the only one who gave *me* any pleasure.

23

BRI: When you first told me that I was knocked out. I walked round for days feeling like a phallic symbol. I thought well, perhaps I didn't ring the bell very often but at least I rang it loud.

(*She smiles.*)

She'll stick with me, I went on happily, because I've got magic super-zoom with added cold-start.

SHEILA: You have, yes.

BRI: Till Freddie——

SHEILA: O ye Gods——

BRI: Of all people!

SHEILA: He's never been near me.

BRI: I think we should still be honest. Even about him.

SHEILA: He leaves me cold.

BRI: And yet you'd rather spend the evening with him than me.

SHEILA: You pushed me into this drama lark. You said I should get out——

BRI: What's his speciality? His forté. Does he keep his mac on?

(SHEILA *faces him for several seconds. Then goes off and upstairs.* BRI *shrugs, turns back to the room. Sighs.* JOE *sneezes.*)

Bless you.

(*She sneezes again, falls forward on to the tray and bumps her face.*)

Oops.

(*She begins crying, feebly. He goes to her.*)

Did she hurt? Did she bump her nose? (*Props her up again.*) Better? (*Looks at her closely.*) You look pale, Joe. Is it those nasty fits? Never mind. (*Fondles her hand.*) Lovely soft hands you've got. Like silk. Lady's hands. *They've* never done rough work. (*Crouching by her chair.*) Now. Mum's gone to take her part. Practise her acting. So we'll have a bit of a chinwag round the oil heater. Chew the fat, watch the jumping.

(*Her crying has stopped.*)

I expect there's jumping, there usually is. (*Gets "Radio Times"*) No. No jumping.

(JOE *sighs heavily and wearily, an aftermath of the cry.*)

24

There's a film about an eminent surgeon and his fight against injustice in London's East End. (*He shows her.*) I know you can't resist a doctor. (*Aside, to audience.*) When you think what they did to her! (*Back to* JOE.) But before that, Daddy get her a lovely tea. Joe and Daddy have a lovely tea then Joe have a nice hot bath? Play with her ducks? (*Returning paper to its place, he looks upwards.*) Hear that noise? That's Mummy in the bedroom. Probably taken her dress off now. Might be putting her stockings on. Even changing entirely. Every stitch. Naked, looking at herself in the glass, thinking have I kept my figure? (*Pause. Dwells on image.*) But I'm not running up those stairs three at a time and falling into the bedroom and cringing on the carpet begging her not to go. No fear! I've done all I can without total loss of dignity. I might have known once I got her started on amateur theatricals she'd turn up at every bloody practice. Terrible sense of duty, your mum.
(*Looks at* JOE *lolling in the chair.*)
What am I doing talking to you?
(*Comes front, talks to audience.*)
Might as well be talking to the wall. (*Then, like a front-cloth comic—*) No, but she is a wonderful woman, my wife. That girl upstairs. In the bedroom, off in the wings, wherever she is. No, seriously. (*Drops it, goes on as himself.*) A truly integrated person. Very rare, that is, as you know. Give you an example: she's disturbed by anything, she's not just mentally upset about it, not only miserable, no, she actually grows *ill*. Boils, backache, vomiting. Not pretence. Real sickness. She works as a whole, not in parts. Unlike me, for instance, I'm Instant Man. Get one for Christmas, endless fun. I'm made up as I go along from old lengths of string, fag-ends . . . magazine cuttings, film-clips . . . all stuck together with wodges of last week's school dinner. What I mean, she couldn't *pretend* a passion she doesn't feel. Whereas I can't sustain a passion to the end of the sentence. I start to cry—aaaoo00w! Then I think: are you mad? Who do you think you are, God? And things go clang and wheels fall off and people get hurt—terrible. You must have felt like this—

25

catching yourself in the mirror hamming away. Or somebody says, "My wife's just been run over," and you want to burst out laughing. Well, you may say, why not—if that's the way you feel? But other people don't like it. So I pretend. You saw me pretend with Sheila. I try to guess which emotions appeal to her and then I sink my teeth in. I don't let go until they're bone-dry. Like with Joe there—(*Waves to her.*) All right, are you? Good. I felt all doomy at first but—well—ten years! I just go through the motions now. Sheila—how shall I put it in a way that will prevent a sudden stampede to the exit-doors? Sheila—embraces all living things. She really does. She's simple, so simple she's bound to win in the end. She's a sane enough person to be able to embrace all living creatures. She sits there embracing all live things. I get my hug somewhere between the budgerigar and the stick-insect. Which is the reason for all this smutty talk. Calling attention to myself to make sure I get more than my share. Otherwise I'd have to settle for eyes-front-hands-on-heads and a therapeutic bash once in a blue moon. And I'm too young to die, I tell you!

JOE: Aaah!

BRI: What's the matter, crackpot?

JOE: Aaah!

BRI: Language? You think this is language! I'll introduce you to Scanlon. He'll let you hear some language. (*Aside.*) What a madam! Well. Let's see what she's left for tea.

JOE: Aaaah!
(*Makes revving noises and pushes her chair off to the kitchen. Going out, he struggles with the cats.*)

BRI: Get back, you flea-bitten whores! Get back! (*Shuts door behind him.*)
(*Pause. At least five seconds.*)
(SHEILA *comes on from a corner downstage of the set. She has changed into a dress and is brushing her hair.*)

SHEILA: One of these days I'll hit him. Honestly. (*Brushes hair, looks at audience.*) He thinks because he throws a tantrum I'm going to stay home comforting him and miss the rehearsal and let them all down. He thinks he's only got to

cry to get what he wants. I blame his mother. She gave him
the kind of suffocating love that makes him think the world
revolves around him but because he's too intelligent to
believe it really, he gets into these paddies and depressions.
And when he's in one of those, he'll do anything to draw
attention to himself. That beetle on his face—you saw that.
And all this stuff about Freddie. And yet it was Brian made
me join these amateurs in the first place, he said I needed to
get out more, have a rest from Joe. But she's no trouble. It's
Brian. I don't know which is the greatest baby. Watching
somebody as limited as Joe over ten years, I've begun to feel
she's only one kind of cripple. Everybody's damaged in some
way. There's a limit to what we can do. Brian, for instance,
he goes so far—and hits the ceiling. Just can't fly any higher.
Then he drops to the floor and we get self-pity again . . .
despair. I'm sure, though, if he could go farther—he could
be a marvellous painter. That's another reason I said I'd
join the amateurs: the thought that he'd be forced to go
upstairs several nights a week and actually put paint on
canvas. And even if he *isn't* any good, he seems to need some
work he can be proud of. Something to take his mind off his
jealousy of anyone or anything I take to . . . relatives, friends,
pets . . . even pot-plants. I'm sure it's because they take up
time he thinks I could be devoting to him. And Joe, most of
all, poor love . . . (*She puts brush on table or chair. A thought
brings her back.*) Look, you mustn't assume I feel like this in
the ordinary way. And even when I *am* a bit down, I shouldn't
normally talk about it to a lot of complete strangers. But all
this childish temper over Freddie—this showing-off—it's
more than I can stand, it makes me boil, honestly! Wouldn't
you feel the same? (*Checks her appearance in imaginary
full-length glass.*) That's why I'm telling you all this. A lot of
total strangers. But wouldn't it make *you* boil? Honestly! A
grown man jealous of poor Joe——
(*Breaks off as she sees* BRI *coming from downstage corner.*)
(*They look at each other in silence.*)
BRI: What are you telling them?
SHEILA: What?

27

BRI: I heard you talking.

(SHEILA *picks threads from her clothes.*)

I heard you mention Joe.

(*No answer.* BRI *speaks to audience.*)

Sheila's got a theory about Joe's birth. She doesn't blame the doctors. She blames herself.

SHEILA: I don't say that. I say it wasn't *entirely* the doctors.

BRI (*nodding*): It was because she choked it back.

SHEILA: It was partly that.

BRI: Because she'd slept around.

SHEILA: I think it was partly because I'd been promiscuous, yes, and my subconscious was making me shrink or withdraw from motherhood, all right!

(*Pause. He looks away. She goes on titivating.*)

BRI: That vicar told us it was the devil's doing. Why don't you believe *that*? It's about as brilliant.

SHEILA (*shrugs*): It comes down in the end to what you believe.

BRI: I'll tell you what *I* believe.

SHEILA: I *know* what you believe.

BRI (*points at audience*): They don't. (*To audience.*) I believe the doctor botched it. There was no other cause. (*To* SHEILA.) That specialist said as much, he said it had nothing at all to do with the way you'd lived or whether there was a nut in the family . . . or what kind of fags you smoked . . .

SHEILA: He didn't say the doctor did it either.

(*Pause. He looks at her.*)

BRI: No. You've got a good point there. He didn't mention that, quite true. He didn't say, "Yes, he's a shoddy midwife, my colleague, always was, I'll see he gets struck off the register." Very true. Weakens my argument, that.

SHEILA: Oh, you're so *clever*!

BRI: He'd only say for certain that it was a chance in a million it could happen again.

SHEILA: Mmm. We haven't had an opportunity yet to check on that.

(*Both pause.*)

BRI: It's due to this that Joe lives at home with us.

SHEILA: She's our daughter.

BRI (*to audience*): She was on the way before we married. That feeds the furnace of guilt.

SHEILA: No need to tell them everything.

BRI: It was a white wedding.

SHEILA: For my dad's sake. He was a bell-ringer and always looked forward to the day he'd lead the peal as I left the church. You said you didn't mind.

BRI: I didn't. At the reception afterwards the ringers were the only people worth talking to. All twisted and crippled. Picture them bouncing up and down at the end of their ropes.
(*And he tries a guess at it.*)

SHEILA: We might have taken them for an omen. The baby came six months later. I'd done my exercises and read the antenatal books—mostly the ones that made it seem as simple as having a tooth filled.

BRI: But more spiritual.

SHEILA: Oh, yes, a lot about you sitting by the bed holding my hand and looking sincere.
(BRI *does it.*)

BRI: Giving the lead with shallow breathing. (*Does it.*)

SHEILA (*to audience*): I don't know whether any of you are like me, but I half-expected to hear snatches of the Hallelujah Chorus.

BRI: I was sympathetic but queasy. The idea of sharing the birth seemed irrefutable *qua idea* . . . but not so gay when it came to the blood and fluid.

SHEILA: As it happened, you needn't have worried.

BRI: No. (*To audience.*) How long do *your* labours last? Two, three hours? A day? Dilettantes! (*Points at* SHEILA.) Five days!

SHEILA: Yes. From the first show on the sheets to the last heave of the forceps. Five days.

BRI: You'll all be saying, "He should have *done* something," but I didn't *know* at the time. You don't, do you?

SHEILA: You'd know *now*.

BRI: Oh, yeah. It was all good experience.

SHEILA (*to audience*): This doctor kept on drugging me.

BRI: You were stoned.

29

SHEILA: I couldn't remember the exercises.

BRI: Couldn't even tell me. Just kept crying.

SHEILA (*explaining*): I couldn't make anyone understand! I couldn't salivate or swallow so I stayed hungry . . . also I kept hoping you'd be there when I opened my eyes, but it was always the midwife or your mother.

BRI: Not always!

SHEILA: Nearly always. You were getting drunk outside.

BRI: What else could I do?

SHEILA (*to audience*): My speech faculties seemed to have gone so I couldn't tell them to stop the dope so that I could manage the birth.

(*For the rest of this act, they hold a dialogue with each other and the audience. No further indication is given, unless essential to the sense.*)

BRI: Then the G.P. would pop in to see me with his boyish grin . . . "Tell the truth I've got the feeling this young shaver's none too keen to join us." And I'd say, "All this trouble getting out and he'll spend the rest of his life trying to get back in." And we'd all piss ourselves at that and have another Scotch.

SHEILA: You never thought it was going on too long?

BRI: Yes, but you leave it to them, don't you? My mum taught me to believe in doctors and during the labour she set an example of quiet faith.

SHEILA: And afterwards—when Joe was ill—she said she knew all the time it was lasting too long.

BRI: She always knows afterwards.

SHEILA: The pain was shocking but the worst was not being able to speak.

BRI: By the last day I thought she was going to die. And—I've never told you this, love——

SHEILA: What?

BRI: You'll find it hard to credit this. Though not normally a religious man . . . for everyday purposes making the usual genuflections to Esso Petroleum and M.G.M.—I don't mind admitting it, I prayed——

SHEILA: Did you really? Not another joke?

BRI: No, honestly, I went down on my knees and I prayed to God.

I said, "God, I've only just found her. The baby doesn't matter. If it's a question of a swop . . ."

SHEILA: Aaaah! (*She kisses him.*)

BRI: Then I found I was so drunk I could hardly get to my feet again.

SHEILA: But never mind, your prayer was answered.

BRI: Yes, He heard all right. (*To audience.*) I see Him as a sort of manic depressive rugby-footballer. He looked down and thought to Himself, "I'll fix that bastard." (*Shakes his fist at roof.*) And He did!

SHEILA: By the time the damage was done, they took me to hospital. The next I knew, they handed me this hairless yellow baby with forceps-scars all over her scalp. She was gorgeous. By the time I got her home, the scars and jaundice were gone and she was in working order. You had a cold.

BRI: That's right, yes.

SHEILA: I had to look after you. It was better than having you turn up every day moaning and sniffling.

BRI: More than a cold. 'Flu. A delayed action I think it must have been. I was quite poorly.

(*She smiles, then goes on to audience.*)

SHEILA: Soon I began to notice these funny turns. We asked our friends who'd had babies but they said it was most likely wind. So in the end we took to her our new G.P.

(BRI *has fetched a tubular cushion from the set behind them, which is now in semi-darkness. The cushion is the size and shape of a swaddled baby.* SHEILA *nurses it.*)

BRI: Baby. (*Points to himself.*) Doctor. Nice, bone-headed.

(*In the sketches which follow,* BRI *plays the funny men and* SHEILA *herself. They do it as they might repeat the dialogue from a favourite film. Sometimes they improvise, surprising or corpsing each other.*)

(BRI *mimes opening a door at side of stage.* SHEILA *wanders off to opposite side and waits.*)

Bye-bye, Mrs.—um—you rub that in you'll soon be as right as rain. (*Mimes closing door, returns to centre, shouts.*) Next, please!

(SHEILA *moves in.* BRI *bends over writing and putting away last*

31

patient's card. Has his back to SHEILA.)

'Evening, Mister—um—feeling any better?

SHEILA: It's morning, Doctor. (*To audience.*) Not very reassuring.

BRI: 'Course it is.

SHEILA: And I've never been before.

BRI: No?

SHEILA: We're new to the district.

BRI: What seems to be the trouble?

SHEILA: I don't really know. Funny turns. Face-making.

BRI: Say "aaah".

SHEILA: Not me. The baby.

(BRI *looks at the cushion.*)

BRI: Nothing much wrong with this little laddie.

SHEILA: Lassie.

BRI: Lassie. Funny turns, you say. How would you describe them?

SHEILA: Frightening.

BRI: No, I meant, what form do they take?

SHEILA: Blinking with her eyes, working with her tongue, shaking
her head, then going all limp.

BRI (*tickling the baby, talking to it*): Funny turns indeed at your
age! Saucy beggar. We are not amused.

SHEILA: But what d'you think it is?

BRI: Wind.

SHEILA: That's what our friends said.

BRI: Always wise to get a second opinion. Have you tried Gripe
Water?

SHEILA: Yes, of course.

BRI: My old mother used to swear by it. Cure anything, she used
to say. Well, let's see what we can find in here.

(*Rummages in drawer, finds medicine, reads label.*)

Ah, yes, this'll put a stop to it. Came in the post this morning.
The makers praise it very highly.

SHEILA: Doctor—I wish you could *see* one of these turns.

BRI: Oh, I've seen them, dear. Got three great monsters of my
own.

SHEILA: I am sorry.

BRI: What?

SHEILA: All your children being—um——

BRI: No, I mean great thriving brutes. Not monsters, no. Your first, is it? First baby?

SHEILA: Yes.

BRI: Well, dear, it's like this. You're throwing an awful lot of gubbins down the old cake-hole there. It's like running in a new car. Till all the tappets and contact breakers get adjusted to the absolute thou, you take it easy, give 'em a chance. Same with these chaps. (*Tickles the cushion, looks again at medicine.*) Let's see. Three times daily after meals. How often you feeding?

SHEILA: Every four hours.

BRI: Fours into twenty-four goes six. So six times a day——

SHEILA: Look. This may be one now.

(*They watch the cushion for ten seconds.* BRI *looks at his watch.*)

SHEILA: No.

BRI: I've got a waiting-room full of people, dear. You try her with this and come back if there's no improvement in—say—a week. Make sure you wind her well. And don't fret. (*Leading her to exit.*) They're hardy little devils, you know. Bye-bye, Mrs.—um—(*Mimes seeing her off and shuts the door.*) Three days later. (*Mimes opening door and calls.*) Next, please. (SHEILA *comes back at once with cushion.*) Hullo, Mrs.—um——

SHEILA (*urgently*): Doctor——

BRI: Just a minute, I'll get your card.

SHEILA: But this child——

BRI: Sit down, please.

(*He seats her and looks at card.*) Didn't I say come back in a week? Why so soon?

SHEILA: She's gone into a coma.

BRI: D'you try the medicine?

SHEILA: She won't take anything. She hasn't fed for two days.

(BRI *looks at the cushion, listens to it, claps hands by it, finally shakes it like a piggy-bank.*)

BRI (*as much as to say "so far, so good"*): Ah-ha! Mm-hum. (*Goes humming back to the table, mimes dialling.*) Get me the Children's Hospital . . . quick! No panic, dear, just a routine inquiry. Your husband with you?

33

SHEILA: He's in the waiting-room. Is she——?

BRI (*into phone*): Look—I'd like you to take a shufti at a baby—uh—(*To* SHEILA.) Girl?

SHEILA: Yes.

BRI: Baby girl . . . Off her chow and failing to respond to any stimuli whatever. (*To* SHEILA *again*.) Got a car?

SHEILA: No.

BRI: Hullo? . . . No car. Any chance of an ambulance? . . . Understood.

(*Puts down phone, returns to* SHEILA.)

SHEILA: There's something seriously wrong, isn't there?

BRI: Don't start worrying, dear. Look at it this way. You know when you get a starter-motor jammed? Seems serious at the time but put it in second gear and rock the whole shoot back and forth, she's soon as right as rain.

SHEILA: We haven't got a car, I——

BRI: What I want you to do—you know the kiddies' hospital? (*She nods.*)

You and your old man go along there—not forgetting to take the baby—you catch a bus from the end of the street. And—*nil desperandum.*

(*Sees her to door, as before, opens it, pushes her through. Is about to close it when he remembers something and shouts after her.*)

Thirty-two.

SHEILA: What?

BRI: The bus. Number thirty-two.

SHEILA: Oh.

BRI (*closing door, taking out handkerchief, wiping brow*): Strewth.

SHEILA (*turning to audience*): On the bus I said to Brian, "I've got a feeling we shan't bring her back." But, as you know, we did. Eventually.

BRI: Every cloud has a jet-black lining.

SHEILA: I stayed in hospital with her for a few weeks, then left her there having tests and came home to look after Brian, who'd contracted impetigo.

(BRI, *in the shadows, lights a cigarette.*)

It was painful not feeding so Brian knelt in front of me and

34

tried to express it orally.

BRI: You should have seen that—like the Kama Sutra.

SHEILA: In the end, a woman from the clinic drew it off with a sort of glass motor-horn.

(BRI *gets a coffee-table from the set, puts the cushion on it, stands behind it.*)

Few weeks later they called me to collect Joe from hospital, by which time we'd gathered that she wasn't ever going to amount to much. But I was determined to know the best we could expect. And the worst. The pediatrician was German —or Viennese, I'm not too sure.

(*For this sketch,* BRI *uses a music-hall German accent.*)

BRI: Vell, mattam, zis baby off yours has now been soroughly tested and ve need ze bets razzer battly so it's better you take her home. I sink I can promise she von't be any trouble. Keep her vell sedated you'll hartly know she's zere.

SHEILA: But, Doctor——

(*He is making for the door, turns reluctantly.*)

BRI: Ja?

SHEILA: Can't you tell me the results?

BRI: Results?

SHEILA: Of the tests.

BRI: Vitch ones? Zere vere so many—(*Slight laugh. Lists on fingers.*) Electro-encephalograph, scree-dimensional eggs-ray, blood urine and stool analyses, zis business vis needles in ze fontanelle——

SHEILA: Is that why her hair's been shaved off?

BRI: Vell of course——

SHEILA: She'd only just begun to grow it. And did the needles make that scar on her head?

BRI: Scar?

SHEILA (*pointing*): There.

BRI: Ach, nein. Zis vos a liddle biopsy to take a sample of her brain tissue.

SHEILA: That's a relief. (*She smiles quickly.*) I thought at first you'd bored a hole in her skull to let the devil out.

(BRI *looks interested, confers with his assistant.*)

BRI: Sounds gut. Did you try it? . . . Ah! (*To* SHEILA.) My colleague

says ve don't do zat any more. (*Shrugs.*) Pity! Vell—if you
eggscuse me.
(*Moves to go.*)

SHEILA: But—Doctor, Doctor——

BRI: Donner und blitzen!

SHEILA: What can she *do*?

BRI: Do? She can't do nozzing at all.

SHEILA: Will she ever?

BRI: Mattam, let me try and tell you vot your daughter iss like.
Do you know vot I mean ven I say your daughter vos a
wegetable?
(SHEILA *thinks for a moment, gets it, smiles.*)

SHEILA: Yes! You mean "Your daughter was a vegetable".

BRI: Ach himmel! Still is, still *is*, always vill be! I have trouble vis
Englisch werbs.

SHEILA: But—when people say to me what kind of cripple is your
child, shall I say—she's a wegetable—a *v*egetable?

BRI: You vont a vord for her? (*Shrugs.*) You can say she iss a
spastic vis a damaged cerebral cortex, multiplegic, epileptic,
but vis no organic malformation of ze brain.

SHEILA: That *is* a long word.

BRI (*gaily*): Which iss vy I prefer wegetable.

SHEILA: *V*egetable.

BRI: *V*egetable.

SHEILA: But why? If her brain's physically sound, why doesn't it
work?
(BRI *sighs, looks at her, thinks.*)

BRI: Imagine a svitchboard. A telephone svitchboard, ja?

SHEILA: I worked as a switchboard operator once.

BRI: Das ist wunderbar! Vell. Imagine you're sitting zere now,
facing ze board. So?

SHEILA: So.

BRI: Some lines tied up, some vaiting to be used—suddenly
brr-brr, brr-brr——

SHEILA: Incoming call?

BRI: Exactly! You plug in.
(SHEILA *mimes it, assuming a bright telephone voice.*)

SHEILA: Universal Shafting.

BRI (*coming out of character*): What?

SHEILA: That was the firm I worked for.

BRI: You've never put that in before.

SHEILA (*shrugs*): I thought I would this time.

BRI: Universal Shafting? Story of your life.

> (*She stares coldly.* BRI *clears his throat, resumes as doctor.*)
> But at zat moment anozzer incoming call—brr-brr—and you
> panic and plug him in to the first von and leave zem talking
> to each ozzer and you answer an extension and he vont the
> railway station but you put him on to ze cricket results and
> zey all start buzzing and flashing—and it's too much, you
> flip your lid and pull out all the lines. Kaputt! Now zere's
> your epileptic fit. Your Grand or Petit Mal according to ze
> stress, ze number of calls. All right?
>
> (*Makes to go again.*)

SHEILA: But, Doctor, Doctor——

> (*Looks at his watch.*)

BRI: Gott in himmel! I'm wery busy man, Missis—um——

SHEILA: I know you must be——

BRI: Yours isn't ze only piecan in ze country.

SHEILA: I know——

BRI: Zere's von born every eight hours, you know.

SHEILA: No, I didn't. Is that true?

BRI: Oh, ja, ja. Not all as bad as zees case, of course——

SHEILA: Isn't there *any*thing at all we can do?

BRI: But jawohl! You must feed her, vosh her nappies, keep her
    varm. Just like any ozzer mozzer.

SHEILA: But for how long?

BRI: Who can tell? Anysing can happen, you know zat. Diphtheria,
    pneumonia . . . vooping cough . . . Colorado beetle.

> (SHEILA *laughs. They come out of character.*)

SHEILA: Oh, that's terrible. Colorado beetle.

BRI: I only just thought of that.

SHEILA: It's terrible.

BRI: So—what happened then? We brought her home.

SHEILA: And the hospital passed the can back to our local G.P.

BRI: The piecan.

SHEILA: He had to supply phenobarbitone and keep us happy. He

[handwritten at top: switchboard metaphor is supposed to explain the fits, but it fails, it only explains the metaphor itself (the switchboard)]

used to come once a week to explain her fits. In layman's
terms.

BRI: You didn't find out much?

SHEILA: Abouts fits, no. But I learnt a lot about what happens on
a switchboard when the lines get crossed.

BRI: Or at a railway junction during fog.

SHEILA: But the time came when I asked him whose fault it was.

BRI: Which is when he suggested the vicar might call.

SHEILA: Yes. Nice vicar. Sensitive. So concerned and upset at the
sight of Joe—the fits were unusually bad that day—so we
left her in the cot and had our chat in another room.

(*She throws the cushion to* BRI, *who puts its on sofa.*)

(*Quite a long pause while they prepare themselves for the next
scene. The mood changes slightly.* BRI *allows* SHEILA *to take the
initiative and plays the Vicar quietly, even seriously, to begin
with. They go upstage and she brings him down again when they
are ready.*)

Here we are. Do take a pew.

(BRI, *as Vicar, laughs.*)

Oh!

(*She laughs too.*)

BRI: She's a beautiful child.

SHEILA: Yes, isn't she?

BRI: It's tragic. Tell me—when you first—knew there was nothing
to be done, how did you feel?

SHEILA: Well, of course, you find out gradually, not all at once.
But there is a point when you finally accept it. And that's—
(*Shakes her head.*) Oh, very nasty. You think "why me?" I
don't know about the other mothers but *I* kept saying, "Why
me, why us?" all day long. Then you get tired of that and
you say, "Why not me?"

BRI: Indeed. You learn humility. You recognize that we are surely
in a vale of tears and you are no exception.

SHEILA: I recognized that I was worse. I'd been promiscuous, you
see. All kinds of men. It seemed to me I was responsible for
Joe, being punished.

BRI: No, no.

SHEILA: No, I don't mean that either. I held the baby back. Out

38

of guilt.

BRI: Really, my dear, you mustn't believe this. Plenty of women who've slept around afterwards become splendid mothers. Pre-marital intercourse is no longer considered a serious obstacle to being taken into the fold.

SHEILA: No?

BRI: Haven't you read our publications lately? You should. The good old C. of E. is nowadays a far more swinging scene than you seem to suppose.

SHEILA: I see.

BRI: Oh, surely. Where the action is.

SHEILA: I've never committed adultery.

BRI: There you are! That's splendid—fabulous! Crazy! Think no more about it. Tell me, what was your husband's reaction to the child?

SHEILA: He used to say, "Think of something worse." And of course that's easy. Joe could have grown older and developed into a real person before it happened. Or she could have been a very *intell*igent spastic without the use of her limbs. Which is worse, I think, than being a kind of living parsnip.

BRI: Quote. You count your blessings.

SHEILA: Yes.

BRI: And that gives you fortitude.

SHEILA: No, but it's something to do. When you're up against a —disaster of this kind—an Act of God——
(BRI *clears his throat.*)
—it's so *numbing* you feel you must make some sense of it—otherwise—you'd——

BRI: Give up hope?

SHEILA: Yes. My husband doesn't feel the need to make sense of anything. He lives with despair.

BRI (*coming out of character*): Did you tell him that?

SHEILA: Why not?

BRI: Bit saucy.

SHEILA: Well, don't you?

BRI: Can't argue now.

SHEILA (*resuming scene*): He says I shouldn't look for explanations.

39

BRI: He doesn't believe in God?

SHEILA: His own kind of God. A manic-depressive rugby footballer.

BRI: It's a start. Provide some basis for argument.
(*He smiles.*)

SHEILA: He doesn't like me praying.

BRI: You have been praying?

SHEILA: What else can I do? I look at that flawless little body, those glorious eyes, and I pray for some miracle to—get her started. It seems, if we only knew the key or the combination, we could get her moving. D'you think the story of the Sleeping Beauty was about a spastic?

BRI: Who can say indeed? (*He stands, moves about.*) My dear, your child's sickness doesn't please God. In fact, it completely brings Him down.

SHEILA: Why does He allow it then?

BRI: How can we know?

SHEILA: Then how can you know it doesn't please Him?

BRI: We can't know. Only guess. It may be disease and infirmity are due to the misuse of the freedom He gave us. Perhaps they exist as a stimulus to research.

SHEILA: Research?

BRI: Against infirmity and disease.

SHEILA: But if He didn't permit disease, we shouldn't need research.

BRI: But He does so we do.
(*She sighs, shakes her head.*)
My dear, the Devil is busy day and night. God does His best but we don't help Him much. Now and then some innocent bystander blunders into the cross-fire between good and evil and——
(*Makes gunfire noises, ricochet-sounds, falls elaborately clutching his chest. Stands again, dusts himself down, before proceeding.* SHEILA *watches calmly.*)
Or—if you can imagine a poisonous blight that settles on an orchard of many different varieties of tree——

SHEILA: No, please, no more parables. I've had so many from the doctor!

40

BRI: But how can I explain without imagery of——

SHEILA: I misled you. I don't want explanations. I've asked the people who should have been able to explain and they couldn't.

BRI: What *do* you want?

SHEILA: Magic.

BRI: I was slowly coming round to that. Once or twice, over the years, we have had in this parish children like your daughter.

SHEILA: Just as bad?

BRI: Oh, yes, I'm sure, quite as bad. Now for those poor innocents I did the Laying On Of Hands bit.

SHEILA: What is that?

BRI: A simple ceremony in your own home. A few prayers, a hymn or two, a blessing, an imposition of hands. Nothing flashy.

SHEILA: Who'd be there?

BRI: You, your husband, anyone you chose.

SHEILA: My husband?

BRI: Yes. And it sounds as though he needs instruction. His prayers would hardly help us if addressed to a manic-depressive rugby footballer.

SHEILA: No.

BRI: God might feel affronted.

SHEILA: Yes.

BRI: He's only human. No, He's not, how silly of me!

SHEILA: Perhaps you could have a word with him. Over a pint.

BRI: Ah, with your husband, yes. Not that there's anything wrong with rugby. Scrum-half myself for years. Just that I feel one shouldn't make a religion of it.

SHEILA: With the other children—did you have any luck? Did God —you know——

BRI: There was one boy—no better than Joe—made such rapid recovery after I'd done the Laying On a few times—the medicos confessed themselves bewildered. He's twelve now and this spring he was runner-up in the South West Area Tap-Dancing Championships.

SHEILA: How fantastic!

(BRI *begins dancing and singing.*)

41

BRI : Happy Feet, I've got those Happy Feet,
Give me a low down beat——
(*Dances and sings without words. Then stops.*)
SHEILA : D'you really think you could—work a miracle?
BRI : Not me, my dear. If a miracle happens, it's only *through* me.
But remember Jairus's daughter—"Damsel, I say unto thee,
arise." Who knows? Perhaps in a few years' time we shall see
little Joe——
(*Dances and sings again.*)
Animal crackers in my soup
Lions and tigers loop the loop.
SHEILA (*standing, breaking out of sketch*): But you wouldn't do it!
(*She moves away.* BRI *drops his Vicar imitation.*)
He was a good man, kind and sincere.
BRI : He was, yes.
SHEILA : And that boy was cured.
BRI : Certainly improved. And, yes, he was the runner-up in the
South West Area Tap Dancing Championships. *But.* He
never *had* been as bad as Joe.
SHEILA : I don't care——
BRI : I looked into it——
SHEILA : You shouldn't have.
BRI : I spoke to people——
SHEILA : Where's the harm? What else did we have?
BRI : Nothing.
SHEILA : Well!
BRI : I'd rather have nothing than a lot of lies.
SHEILA : You're unusual.
BRI : First he'd have done it for us, then he'd have got a few of
his mates in to give the prayers more Whoosh! More Pow!
And before long he'd have had us doing it in church
gloated over by all those death-watch beetles like the
victims of a disaster.
SHEILA : It could have worked. He might have magicked her.
BRI : I'm sure it was best to stop it then than later on—after he'd
raised your hopes. Sheila——
(*She looks at him, smiles.*)
Anyway. If the vicar had got her going, she'd only have had

42

one personality. As it is, we've given her dozens down the years.

SHEILA (*to audience*): As soon as we were admitted to the free-masonry of spastics parents, we saw she had even less character than the other children. So we began to make them for her.

BRI: Some never really suited.

SHEILA: No. Like the concert pianist dying of t.b.

BRI: Nor the girl who was tragically in love with a darkie against her parents' wishes.

SHEILA: That was based on "Would you let your daughter marry one?"

BRI: I used to like the drunken bag who threw bottles at us if we didn't fetch her gin and pipe-tobacco.

SHEILA: But they were all too active. The facial expression wasn't right.

BRI: The one that's stuck is the coach-tour lady . . . powder-pink felt hat, white gloves, Cuban heel shoes, swagger-coat . . .

SHEILA: And seasick pills in her handbag just in case there's a lot of twisting and turning.

BRI: She hates foreigners——

SHEILA: And council-houses——

BRI: And shafting. She knows to her cost what that can lead to.

SHEILA: Loves the Queen——

BRI: And Jesus. She sees him as an eccentric English gentleman. Sort of Lawrence of Arabia.

SHEILA: Very disapproving of pleasure.

BRI: Not *all* pleasure. A nice Julie Andrews film with tea after——

SHEILA: Tea in the Odeon cafe——

BRI: Nothing nicer. Which reminds me. I'm supposed to be giving her tea. In this play we started doing.
(*Looks at his watch.*)

SHEILA: We got side-tracked.

BRI: She'll have something to say to me. She'll have me on the carpet. "Nice thing leaving the table before you've finished eating, leaving me stuck here like Joe Egg . . ."
(*Goes off.*)
(SHEILA *watches him out of sight.*)

43

SHEILA: I join in these jokes to please him. If it helps him live with her, I can't see the harm, can you? He hasn't any faith she's ever going to improve. Where I have, you see . . . I believe, even if she *showed* improvement, Bri wouldn't notice. He's dense about faith—faith isn't believing in fairy-tales, it's being in a receptive state of mind. I'm always on the look-out for some sign . . . (*Looks off again to wings to make sure* BRI'*s not coming.*) One day when she was—what?—about a twelve month old, I suppose, she was lying on the floor kicking her legs about and I was doing the flat. I'd made a little tower of four coloured bricks—plastic bricks—on a rug near her head. I got on with my dusting and when I looked again I saw she'd knocked it down. I put the four bricks up again and this time watched her. First her eyes, usually moving in all directions, must have glanced in passing at this bright tower. Then the arm that side began to show real signs of intention . . . and her fist started clenching and—spreading with the effort. The other arm—held there like that—(*raises one bent arm to shoulder level*) didn't move. At all. You see the importance—she was using for the first time one arm instead of both. She'd seen something, touched it and found that when she touched it whatever-it-was was changed. Fell down. Now her bent arm started twitching towards the bricks. Must have taken—I should think—ten minutes'—strenuous labour—to reach them with her fingers . . . then her hand jerked in a spasm and she pulled down the tower. (*Reliving the episode, she puts her hands over her face to regain composure.*) I can't tell you what that was like. But you can imagine, can't you? Several times the hand very nearly touched and got jerked away by spasm . . . and she'd try again. That was the best of it—she had a will, she had a mind of her own. Soon as Bri came home, I told him. I think he said something stupid like—you know—"That's great, put her down for piano lessons." But when he tested her—putting piles of bricks all along the circle of her reach—both arms—and even sometimes out of reach so that she had to stretch to get there—well, of course, he saw it was true. It wasn't *much* to wait for—one arm movement completed—

44

and even that wasn't sure. She'd fall asleep, the firelight would distract her, sometimes the effort would bring on a fit. But more often than not she'd manage . . . and a vegetable couldn't have done that. Visitors never believed it. They hadn't the patience to watch so long. And it amazed me—I remember being stunned—when I realized they thought I shouldn't deceive myself. For one thing, it wasn't deception . . . and, anyway, what else could I do? We got very absorbed in the daily games. Found her coloured balls and bells and a Kelly —those clowns that won't lie down. Then she caught some þug and was very sick . . . had fit after fit—the Grand Mal, not the others—what amounted to a complete relapse. When she was over it, we tried the bricks again, but she couldn't even seem to see them. That was when Bri lost interest in her. I still try, though of course I don't bother telling him. I'll tell him when something happens. It seems to me only common sense. If she did it once, she could again. I think while there's life there's hope, don't you? (*Looks to wings again.*) I wish he'd talk more seriously about her. I wonder if he ever imagines what she'd be like if her brain worked. *I* do. And Bri's mother always says, "Wouldn't she be lovely if she was running about?" which makes Bri hoot with laughter. But I think of it too. Perhaps it's being a woman. (*Lights off* SHEILA. *Lights on set upstage, very strong like a continuous lightning flash.*)

(JOE *skips on, using a rope.*)

JOE: Mrs. D, Mrs. I, Mrs. FFI, Mrs. C, Mrs. U, Mrs. LTY
Mrs. D, Mrs. I, Mrs. FFI, Mrs. C, Mrs. U, Mrs. LTY.
(*Stops skipping.*)
Ladies and gentlemen, there will now be an interval. Afterwards the ordinary play, with which we began the performance, will continue and we shall try to show you what happens when Sheila returns home with their mutual friends, Freddie and Pam. Thank you.
(*She bows and resumes skipping.*)

ACT TWO

Darkness.

   SHEILA *opens hall door and looks in, light behind her.*

SHEILA: No. (*Comes in, puts on lights.*) Not in here. Must be
   working. Miracles never cease.

   (FREDDIE *and* PAM *follow in. He is suited, school-tied, with a
   hearty barking humourless laugh, same age as* BRI *but his
   ample public confidence makes him seem middle-aged.*)

   (PAM *dresses well, mispronounces her words in an upper-class
   gabble and her postures and manners have been taken from
   fashionable magazines. She uses this posture to hold her own
   against* FREDDIE's *heartiness.*)

FREDDIE: Not here?

SHEILA: Must be working in the attic.

PAM: Or gone to bed.

FREDDIE: At ten o'clock?

SHEILA: Perhaps hiding? (*She looks about the room behind various
   pieces of furniture.*)

   (FREDDIE *and* PAM *look at each other.*)

   No. Working.

PAM: Gorgeous room.

SHEILA: Oh, Pam, no!

PAM: Absolutely gorgeous. Not the room so much, what you've
   done with it.

SHEILA: Cost absolutely nothing.

PAM: It's terribly P.L.U. Isn't it, darling?

SHEILA: How's that?

PAM: P.L.U. People Like Us. That dresser, for instance——

SHEILA: Twelve and six.

PAM: No!

SHEILA: In a country sale.

PAM: Absolutely gorgeous. I'm green, aren't you, darling?

FREDDIE: Yes, but how many coats of paint did you take off?

46

SHEILA: Three. Cream, brown and green.

PAM: Lord, the plebs and their lavatory colours.

SHEILA: Freddie, you don't feel I bullied you?

FREDDIE: What?

SHEILA: Into coming back here? Sit down, do.

FREDDIE: No. Why?

SHEILA: I feel I did. Carrying on like that. Crying. I've been going hot and cold ever since. Don't tell Bri, will you?

FREDDIE. What?

SHEILA: How I cried.

FREDDIE: Not if you say so.

SHEILA: Please. How d'you like your coffee?

FREDDIE: Half-and-half. It's nothing to be——

SHEILA: Pam? Half-and-half?

PAM: Black, please.

FREDDIE: Nothing to be ashamed of. Wish I knew how to give way more to *my* emotions. Must be years since my water-works were turned on.

PAM: Hope so too.

FREDDIE: It's an enviable capacity.

PAM: Gives me the creeps, a man in tears.

FREDDIE: That's why you can give so much on the stage.

SHEILA: Was it all right tonight?

FREDDIE: All right? Was it all right? A bit more than *all right*, duckie.

SHEILA: No, truly.

FREDDIE: Truly. An electric evening.

SHEILA: It felt awful.

FREDDIE: Pam, you saw it. Was it awful?

PAM: Gorgeous, you were absolutely gorgeous.

SHEILA: It's a lovely part.

FREDDIE: You draw on deep wells of compassion.

SHEILA: You are sweet.

(*He kisses her hand.* SHEILA, *embarrassed, smiles at* PAM *as though to include her.* PAM *smiles back.*)

(SHEILA *goes off upstage and calls up the stairs*). Bri! I'm making coffee, if you want some. (*Shuts door behind her.*)

(FREDDIE *looks at cowboy paintings, as though he thought of*

47

buying one.)
(*Pause.*)
(PAM *looks at him.*)

FREDDIE: Clever these. (*Barks.*) Done by Brian, you know.

PAM: That was good—about bullying you.

FREDDIE: What?

PAM: I nearly fell about when she said that.

FREDDIE: 'Fraid I'm not with you.

PAM: Bully you! You were so damned keen to get in here you fell out of the car!

(FREDDIE *looks back at paintings, pauses, moves away.*)

FREDDIE: I fell from the car because my ankle was caught in the safety belt.

(PAM *laughs. She has opened her bag and taken out a cigarette.*)

Go on. Piss yourself.

PAM: Don't be coarse.

FREDDIE: That yob on the motor-bike nearly went over me.

PAM: Give me a match, will you?

FREDDIE: I thought you wanted to *help* these people.

PAM: Not me, darling.

FREDDIE: They need help. We can afford to give it. (*Lights cigarette.*) You've been smoking like a furnace all night.

PAM: And all day. I always smoke when I'm bored.

FREDDIE: If you're bored, go home. Your car's outside.

PAM: I'm bored there too. All day.

FREDDIE: Then interest yourself in someone else. Sheila, for instance. We've done a lot for Sheila, darling. We mustn't stop now.

PAM: You, not me.

FREDDIE (*explaining, to audience*): Well, I'm not the sort to sit around making sympathetic noises and doing sweet F.A., so naturally as soon as I heard she'd been on the stage I saw the way to help. Got her down to join the players: friendly crowd, nice atmosphere . . . worked like a dose of salts. So well in fact, poor old Bri's gone slightly hatcha—thinks I'm getting my end away with Sheila.

PAM: Hardly surprising. He's left holding the baby.

FREDDIE: Exactly.

PAM: Literally.

FREDDIE: Yes, tragic. Which is why I'm here. (a) To tell him there's nothing in it. (b) Get them both to see sense about the poor kiddie. And (c) to give poor Brian back an interest in life.

(PAM *makes a face, looks at her watch.*)

PAM: It's gone ten now. What sort of thing had you got in mind?

FREDDIE: What for?

PAM: To give him back an——

FREDDIE: Ah. I thought for a starter, get him down to see his wife in the play.

PAM: Of course you're joking.

FREDDIE: No.

PAM: You told me he can't stand acting.

FREDDIE: Part of his chosen image. If he *loves* the woman—and he *claims* he does——

PAM: She's not even any *good* in it.

FREDDIE: Will you shut up! (*Looks nervously towards kitchen.*)

(PAM *did not lower her voice.*)

(*Pause.*)

(FREDDIE *moves again, like a cross father.*)

PAM: Well, is she? He'll see in a flash you're giving her charity and he's hardly the kind of man who——

FREDDIE: I think I know him a shade better than you. We were at *school* together.

PAM: Same school at the same time. I wouldn't exactly call that "together".

FREDDIE (*to audience*): Some truth in that. He was always in the backward classes. Spent his time in the back rows farting and so forth——

PAM: Freddie!

FREDDIE: And there was no need for it, he was brainy enough. Just got in with the wrong crowd. No, that sounds reactionary but you've only got to look at him. Half-way through his life and no degree, no future, not much past . . . coping with the arse-end of a comprehensive school and driving a fifteen-year-old Popular.

(SHEILA *enters from kitchen.*)

SHEILA: Ginger cat didn't come in here?

PAM: Haven't seen it.

(SHEILA *makes to go.*)

Want helping?

SHEILA: No, thanks.

(FREDDIE *scratches his arm.* SHEILA *looks at him.* PAM *scratches her thigh.* SHEILA *goes.*)

FREDDIE: Not that my position's anything to boast about. I just took over the factory where Dad left off.

PAM: Oh, not quite, darling. You've worked wonders.

FREDDIE: Only because I'm dead keen. But I'm not as bright as Brian, not nearly as talented. That's what's so galling to me as a Socialist. The waste! Since school, as a matter of fact, I saw nothing of him till six months ago. On a train to Town. I leaned over and said, "Dum spiro spero mean anything to you?"

PAM: Must say it doesn't to me.

FREDDIE: Our school motto. While I live I hope.

PAM: Bit squaresville, darling.

FREDDIE (*stoutly*): I *am* a bit squaresville! Anyway—(*continues to audience*)—he couldn't get away and we had a good old belly-ache. Told me all about his poor kiddie and how Sheila was obsessed with her and how keen he was to get her back in the swim.

PAM: Sheila.

FREDDIE (*bewildered*): Yes.

PAM: Not the weirdie.

FREDDIE: The what?

PAM: You know.

(*Pause.*)

FREDDIE: Don't call her a weirdie, darling.

PAM: I know, darling, it's absolutely horrid. But she is, though, isn't she?

(*Pause.*)

FREDDIE: Try to imagine that one of ours has turned out like that.

50

PAM (*shocked*): Darling! They're absolutely gorgeous, how could you?

(*Pause.* FREDDIE *gives up, returns to audience.*)

FREDDIE: I don't want to sound authoritarian or fascist but there's only one useful approach to any human problem and that's a positive one. No use saying: "This is no way to live, in every night with a hopeless cripple." No use at all. Same with problem teenagers. You don't say, "Naughty boy, go stand in the corner." You say, "Get hold of these nails and a hammer!" Then you're in business.

(*Door opens and* FREDDIE *turns to meet a large portrait of a cowboy, life-size, something like an old photograph. It is pushed on sideways through the slightly opened door. From behind it comes a hand holding a revolver. Shoots off caps.* FREDDIE *barks with laughter.* BRI *comes from behind picture, brings it right in, closes door. He is in painting clothes.*)

FREDDIE: Well, well!

BRI: Nice surprise, Fred. Hullo, Pam. Nice having company. Stuck in here every night like Joe Egg.

PAM: Like who?

BRI: Joe Egg. My grandma used to say, "Sitting about like Joe Egg," when she meant she had nothing to do.

FREDDIE: We've been here ages. Didn't you hear?

BRI: I was miles away.

FREDDIE: In the attic. Sheila said you——

BRI: In the saloon. Painting Wild Bill Hickok. Posed for this just before his last poker game. They got him in the back. Look at his pose. He fancied himself.

FREDDIE: Very good. It really is. Very good. Witty. (*Laughs.*) And this one—from the same series? (*Points to one on the wall.*)

BRI: Ah. That's a story picture. "Where's the sodding bugle-call?" The beleaguered fort holding out for the cavalry that never comes. Few rounds left, Sioux closing in. Inset: cavalryman polishing his harness, smiling for the recruiting posters.
(*Turns up his nose at it.*) Bit preachy.

FREDDIE: Why not? If it's a message that needs——

BRI: Rather have the pure heroic image myself. Like this one.
(*Moves to the third.*) The Thalidomide Kid. Fastest gun in the

West. On the slightest impulse from his rudimentary arm-stumps, the steel hands fly to the holsters, he spins on solid rubber tyres and—pschoo! (*He blazes away.*)

FREDDIE: That's a bit too sick for me.

(BRI *props the picture against the wall.* FREDDIE *moves away.* BRI *comes down to audience, circling.*)

Give me a good message any time.

BRI (*to audience*): What's he doing here? (*To* FREDDIE.) I meant to do Geronimo tonight but Joe had to be—um—attended to—and——

(SHEILA *comes in with four cups.*)

—by the time I'd got her to bed, it hardly seemed worth blacking up.

SHEILA: You've been painting.

BRI (*defensively*): I wore my old clothes.

SHEILA: Brian, fancy saying that! I want you to paint. That's the only reason I take these parts.

BRI: How did it go—the practice?

FREDDIE: Oh, blood, sweat and tears, you know, but it's coming.

SHEILA: Did you mention Joe?

BRI: I said I had to attend to her.

SHEILA: You mean the usual?

BRI: Got some drink, haven't we?

SHEILA: Brian!

BRI (*looking in cupboard*): What?

SHEILA: You mean the usual?

BRI: Bit more than usual.

SHEILA: What d'you mean?

BRI: Cyprus sherry or Spanish cognac. Christ!

SHEILA (*shouts*): Brian!

(*He stares.*)

What d'you mean by more than usual?

BRI (*shouts*): We had a row. She flounced out and slammed the door.

SHEILA: No silly jokes. She's all right?

BRI: I'd rather not talk about it. Here we are—all set for a civilized conversation and you keep on about *that* poor crackpot. Spanish cognac, Fred?

52

FREDDIE (*embarrassed, slightly angry*): Thank you.

BRI: Sheila's parents brought it back from Torremolinos. Sure you wouldn't sooner have cider?

FREDDIE: No. Why?

BRI: I just remembered you're a Socialist. So many places you've got to boycott. Worse than entertaining an R.C.

FREDDIE: I don't go in for that. Misguided. A blow against Fascism, Apartheid? Very likely! All you hurt is some poor peasant.

(*Drinks poured and given out.*)

BRI: Spanish cognac with instant coffee. High life on a teacher's pay.

(*Sits and drinks.*)

SHEILA: Brian, your shoes!

BRI: What?

SHEILA: You wore your teaching shoes and look, they're covered in paint.

BRI: Oh, God!

SHEILA: Just look at them! Freddie, what would Pam say if you got paint on your office shoes?

BRI: I'm sorry, honest, love.

SHEILA: You can't get it off!

BRI: I'll get it off.

SHEILA: Why don't you *think*? Go and change them, go on.

BRI: It's done now. And I'm not painting any more.

SHEILA: Honestly.

(*Pause.*)

As though you couldn't have changed your shoes.

(*Pause. They drink.*)

FREDDIE: How *is* teaching?

BRI: Oh, we keep them off the streets, you know. Eyes front hands on heads.

FREDDIE: You still don't like it?

BRI: It's not exactly Good-bye Mister Chips.

FREDDIE: All the same I envy you. Really. In many ways I often wish I'd been a teacher.

BRI: Instead of a rich and powerful industrialist, yes, it must be lonely.

53

(SHEILA *laughs to remove the sting.*)

FREDDIE (*barking*): Rich? Where d'you get the idea I'm rich.

PAM: We're not *rich*.

SHEILA: Comfortable?

PAM: Comfortable, yes, not rich.

FREDDIE: Nor powerful! (*Barks.*) You've been watching too much telly. No, hamstrung's nearer the mark. I'm like a last-ditch colonial running things till the natives have got enough know-how to take the reins.

BRI: That's right? (*Tut-tuts at the thought.*) Don't know what the world's coming to.

FREDDIE: How are things on the home front, Bri?

BRI: Oh, much the same, you know.

FREDDIE: Stuck in like Joe Egg?

BRI: Yeah.

FREDDIE: Look—perhaps I'm rushing in where angels fear to tread——

PAM: You always do.

(FREDDIE *barks.*)

FREDDIE: But—why don't you see all the doctors money can buy and tell them you want another baby. To put it bluntly—ask why you're not having one.

SHEILA: Oh, we've had fertility counts. That what you mean?

FREDDIE: You've done that?

BRI: Yes. She was A minus, I was B plus. Must concentrate more.

FREDDIE: Well done. I admire your nerve. Most people wouldn't fancy knowing for sure.

SHEILA: No. 'Specially men. Our doctor had an ex-major who turned really nasty when they told him he was sub-fertile. Wouldn't believe it. He kept saying, "But I was in the Normandy landings."

BRI: "I demand a recount."

FREDDIE (*barks with laughter*): Hah! Poor fellow. How absolutely terrifying! How about boosters?

BRI: What?

FREDDIE: Fertility boosters.

SHEILA: No.

FREDDIE: I know a gynaecologist in London, did so well by a

friend of mine his wife's applied to be sterilized.

PAM: Georgina?

FREDDIE: Shall I fix an appointment?

SHEILA: I don't mind.

FREDDIE: If all else fails, I'll get the adoption machinery moving. Takes some time as a rule but I can put some ginger under the right people. Get it moved to the top of the in-tray. Always back out later if you find you've hit the spot.

(SHEILA *winces*.)

So—whatever happens—at least you'll have a proper working child.

SHEILA (*shrugging*): Two children instead of one.

BRI: She won't like it, Mum.

SHEILA: She likes to rule the roost, Dad.

FREDDIE: Surely, my dear, you can see you're only prepared to give up your life to little Joe because there's no one else. Once you've got a normal healthy baby looking up at you, smiling at you—does *she* smile?——

BRI: She used to. Now and then.

SHEILA: Often, often!

FREDDIE: A real baby will smile every time you look at her. And she'll cry too and keep you up every night—and crawl and walk and talk and——

SHEILA: Yes, I've seen them. Then what?

FREDDIE: Well—then—at least you'll be in a position to decide.

SHEILA: What?

FREDDIE: Whether to let Joe go into a residential school.

BRI: We've tried that too.

FREDDIE: Oh?

SHEILA: Putting her away, yes.

FREDDIE: Don't call it that.

SHEILA: What else is it?

BRI: She worried all the time, wouldn't let her stay.

FREDDIE: I'm on the board of a wonderful place. They're not prisons, you know, not these days. They're run by loving and devoted teachers—hideously underpaid, but I'm doing what I can in that direction——

SHEILA: I don't care how good the nurses are—she *knows*! She

55

Freddie is the eternal optimist, to him nothing is insurmountable, which is why he's in play, because he's put up against something so insurmountable as Joe.

was ill in that place.

they retreat into their own world as a way of rejecting Freddie.

rhythm of language between Brian & Sheila like between Didi & Gogo.

BRI: Change of diet.

SHEILA: She was pining.

FREDDIE: This isn't a hospital, it's a special school.

BRI: How's the time going, Pam?

FREDDIE: A private house. Trees all round——

PAM (*to* SHEILA): There was a fabulous article in *Nova* about it. D'you remember?

SHEILA: No.

FREDDIE: And if she improves, she can join their activities——

BRI: Activities?

FREDDIE: Painting . . . wheelchair gardening . . . speech therapy.

BRI: Better not tell *her* that, eh, Mum? She thinks she's very *nicely* spoken. One thing she *does* pride herself on.

SHEILA (*to Freddie*): She wouldn't go to a special school. Not even if you put some ginger under them. We've seen the place she'd go. No private house. No Palladian asylum with acres of graceful parkland.

BRI: Nor Victorian Gothic even.

SHEILA: Army surplus. Like a transit camp.

BRI: Except they're not going anywhere.

SHEILA: Freddie, thanks for trying but it's too late, honestly. I shall have to look after her till she dies.

BRI: Or until you do.

SHEILA: Yes. Whichever's first.

FREDDIE: Is that possible?

SHEILA: What?

FREDDIE: She could outlive you?

SHEILA: We know one—a man of seventy-six, just become a Boy Scout. They said they wouldn't have him any longer in the Cubs.

FREDDIE: These jokes. May I say my piece about these jokes? They've obviously helped you see it through. A useful anaesthetic. But. Isn't there a point where the jokes start using *you*?

SHEILA: I thought you were going to speak to Bri about——

FREDDIE: Please. This first. Isn't that the whole fallacy of the sick joke? It kills the pain but leaves the situation just as it was?

56

Look—when we met again—how many?—six months?—
ago—you used, I remember, a striking metaphor describing
Sheila's state of mind. You said a cataract had closed her
eye—like your mother's net curtains, screening off the world
outside.

BRI: Did I say that?

FREDDIE: It struck me as so bloody apt.

BRI: So bloody smug.

FREDDIE: But it was true, don't you see? And now—in my opinion
—it's all gone arse-over-tip. Sheila's cured and you've caught
the cataract. Shoot me down if I'm all to cock. I'm only
trying to strip it down to essentials. Thinking aloud.

BRI: I wonder—could you think more quietly?

FREDDIE: Am I shouting? Sorry. I tend to raise my voice when I'm
helping people.

BRI: Only my head's splitting.

FREDDIE: All right. (*Sits by* BRI *and addresses him quietly,
earnestly.*) When I see a young couple giving up their lives
to a lost cause, it gives me the screaming habdabs. As a
Socialist! The waste! I think to myself: all right, I don't care,
I *am* my Brother's Keeper, I bloody well am.

BRI: That's much quieter, thanks.
  (*Pause.*)

FREDDIE: Another joke. Another giggle.

PAM: Come on, Freddie, let's go——

FREDDIE: The whole issue's a giggle. I throw you a lifeline and you
giggle. The whole country giggling its way to disaster.

PAM (*to* BRI): She broke down tonight.

BRI: What?

FREDDIE: Pam——

SHEILA: You said you wouldn't——

PAM: In a flood of tears. (*To* FREDDIE.) Come on——

FREDDIE (*taking over*): Because she can't cope any more with your
suspicions and jealousies. So I said I'd put you straight on
one or two points.

PAM: Wasting your breath, darling.

FREDDIE: (a) We're not going to bed together.

BRI (*to* SHEILA): Scab!

57

FREDDIE: (b) It's hardly likely because (a) She loves you, (b) I
love Pam, and (c) I've got three smashing kids——
PAM: Darling, I love you too.
FREDDIE: And I'm hardly likely to throw all that away for a bit on
the side—however gorgeous the bit may be—(*smiling at*
SHEILA)—and though I'm not a practising Christian, I think I
know my duty——
BRI: Yes, but Fred——
FREDDIE: And—squaresville or not—I happen to believe in duty.
PAM: Terribly sweet.
(*They kiss.*)
BRI: I hardly know how to say this now. After your masterly
dismissal of jokes. But—here it is—the whole idea was just
another sick fantasy. I know you've never touched her, leave
alone shafted her.
PAM: He's a nut.
BRI: I wanted to bring back the magic to our marriage. Stir it up,
a kind of emotional aphrodisiac.
PAM: If you ever try that with me, I'll leave you.
FREDDIE: I may be squaresville but I'm not sick.
SHEILA (*to* BRI): You're so round*about*.
BRI: You wouldn't let me near you. All day I'd been running blue
movies on the back of my retina—the pair of us romping
about the bed shouting with satisfaction. And what did I
get?—Your hands are cold.
PAM: This is too juvenile. Let's go.
FREDDIE: That's what he *wants*.
(BRI *gets more drink*.)
But I want to *help* him.
(*Comes to audience.*)
Am I wasting my time, d'you think?
(*Offstage children's voices sing: Once in Royal David's City.*)
BRI: Listen to that. This time of night. How can people hear the
telly?
SHEILA: Oh, she loves the carols. Let me fetch her.
PAM (*showing panic briefly*): No! We're going.
SHEILA: You've never seen her. Wouldn't you like to?
FREDDIE: I'd love to.

58

PAM: It's twenty past ten.

FREDDIE (*shrugs*): The *au-pair* girl will have gone to bed.

PAM: Your train in the morning.

FREDDIE: What train? Not tomorrow——

PAM: I thought it was tomorrow.

FREDDIE: No, darling. You'd like to see her, wouldn't you?

PAM: Love to. Give me a match.

FREDDIE (*barks*): You'll get lung cancer.

PAM (*irritably*): They're my lungs.

(SHEILA *is going.*)

BRI: Sheila—don't.

SHEILA. What?

BRI: I forgot to tell you what happened—while you were out.

(*Pause. She comes back.*)

SHEILA: What?

BRI: Shall I tell you?

SHEILA: Happened where?

BRI: Here. First—I fed Joe. (*To* FREDDIE.) She was constipated. She hadn't been for a week so I chose a nice tin of strained prunes. What my grandma used to call black-coated workers. (*Smiles big show-biz smile expectantly, drops it.*)
They have to be strained still because her teeth are—a bit stumpy . . . after I'd got that lot down, I had a bite myself, read the paper. But she kept having little fits and whimpering so I plonked her in the nursery. I thought to myself, "P'raps the spasm's hurting," so I tried to loosen it with exercises.

SHEILA: The constipation hurts her.

BRI (*explaining to* FREDDIE): The spasm's in the back between the shoulders. Sheila got this method of breaking it down from a lady wrestler she met at an Oxfam coffee party.

SHEILA (*smile to* FREDDIE): A physiotherapist.

BRI: You take her arms and wrap them across her chest—like so —and hold them very tight—then push her head right forward and down till her chin's rammed in between her collar-bones. As though you were trying to make a parcel.
(*Demonstrates.*)
I don't know whether it's any use but I faced the fact long ago that I enjoy it. Find myself smiling when she cries. At

59

least it's a reaction. But tonight she wouldn't stop even when I let her go.

SHEILA: Those fits upset her.

BRI: So I undressed her and applied a suppository. Put a rubber sheet underneath and doubled her up like a book . . . pressed on her stomach to help . . . and at last, over half an hour I think, she managed number twos.

SHEILA: Oh, good. That was bothering her, poor love.

BRI: No, listen a minute. It was no sooner out that she started all that gulping and lip-smacking, stretching her arms, opening and closing her blind eyes . . . the Grand Mal . . . I thought to myself, that's it, the lot! All you can do. Pain and fits. And not for the first time in ten years, I thought: Is it ever worth it?

FREDDIE: It never is.

SHEILA: Worth what?

FREDDIE: The effort.

SHEILA: We've got no choice.

FREDDIE: Of course you have.

BRI: Anyway. When the fit was over I propped her in her chair and stood behind her and put a cushion over her mouth and nose and kept them there while I counted a hundred. There was no struggle or anything. It seemed very—peaceful.

(*The others are watching him, motionless. Pause.*)

SHEILA: What? . . .

PAM: God!

BRI: When it was all over I took the cushion away and . . . I said, "Nurse, you have seen nothing. We are in this together" . . . I looked up to see the nurse throw off her cape revealing the burly figure of Sergeant Blake, Scotland Yard.

SHEILA (*relieved*): Honestly, Brian!

BRI: You almost believed me, didn't you?

FREDDIE: No almost. I *did*.

SHEILA: I should *know* by now. She *is* all right, isn't she?

BRI: Yes.

SHEILA: I'm going to see her.

(*Moving out,* BRI *stops her.*)

BRI: Did you feel relieved at all, even a little bit, when you thought

I'd done it?

SHEILA: Don't be silly.

BRI: Not even a teeny-weeny drop relieved to think it was all over?

SHEILA: How could I? Honestly. (*She goes off and up the stairs.*)

BRI: How about *you*?

FREDDIE: What?

BRI: Were you relieved at all?

FREDDIE: Of course not. Horrified!

BRI: Because it would be murder?

FREDDIE: You can't take life, man.

BRI: Her life—what is it?

FREDDIE: I don't care.

BRI: You've never *seen* her.

FREDDIE: I'd *like* to see her.

BRI: You shall in a minute.

PAM: Darling, it's half past——

BRI (*ignoring her*): She's not alive. What can she *do*?

FREDDIE: It doesn't matter.

BRI: Asphyxiation delayed ten years by drugs.

FREDDIE: She should be put away.

BRI: Everyone's always saying, "Do something," but when I make a suggestion, it's all wrong.

FREDDIE: If all you can suggest is murder, yes.

BRI: Living with Sheila, you get to welcome death. With life burgeoning in every cranny. (*Moves about, listing the wild life.*) Flora, fauna, gawping goldfish . . . budgies . . . busy Lizzie . . . cats . . . cats' fleas . . .

PAM: I *knew* I'd been itching.

BRI: Fleas from Sidney and Beatrice Webb, we're not sure which. When the tom-kitten was born, Sheila wanted to call him Dick, but I drew the line there. Standing on the front steps last thing shouting, "Dick, Dick!" Might have got killed in the rush.

FREDDIE: There are one or two great——

BRI: She embraces all living things. (*To* PAM *hastily:*) Except Freddie. She never embraces him.

FREDDIE: I said there are one or two great moral commandments

61

and in my view they're the only hope we've got against chaos.
Love thine enemy. Thou shalt not kill.

(BRI *lights a cigarette.*)

D'you know how the final solution of the Jewish problem
began? In the mental hospitals. It's only a step from there to
Auschwitz.

BRI : That kind of thing certainly gives legalized killing a bad
name, but—what about the other forms? The bomb-aimer
gets decorated but anyone who lets Joe die gets ten years.

FREDDIE: The cases are different. A rational intelligence can
distinguish between the different cases.

BRI : So I've noticed.

FREDDIE: Put it this way. You don't agree with killing?

BRI (*shrugs*): No.

FREDDIE: But if a madman breaks in here and tries to rape your
wife, what d'you do?

BRI : Kill him.

FREDDIE: Exactly. Killing is sometimes unavoidable.

BRI : Thou shalt not kill unless it's absolutely necessary.

FREDDIE (*doubtfully*): Yes.

BRI (*to audience*): Whose side is he on?

(BRI *smokes. Pause. The singing has ceased.*)

PAM : Darling—it's half past ten.

FREDDIE (*suddenly*): You're like a blasted speaking clock. On the
third stroke—peep-peep-peep.

(*Walks away.*)

PAM : Oh, charming.

(*Looks at both men, ignoring her and now each other. Complete
separation of all three people on the stage.* PAM *comes to
audience.*)

It wasn't my idea coming back here in the first place. But
once Freddie's set eyes on a lame dog, you might as well
talk to the moon. I keep looking at that door and thinking
she's going to come through it any moment with that poor
weirdie. I know it's awful but it's one of my—you know—
THINGS. We're none of us perfect . . . I can't stand anything N.P.A. Non-Physically Attractive. Old women in
bathing-suits—and skin diseases—and cripples . . . Rowton

62

House-looking men who spit and have hair growing out of
their ears . . . No good, I just can't look at them. I know
Freddie's right about Hitler and of course that's horrid.
Still, I can't help sympathizing with Brian, can you? I don't
mean the way he described. I think it should be done by
the state. And so should charity. Then we might have an
end of all those hideous dolls in shop-doorways with irons
on their legs. . . . Freddie won't hear of it, of course. But
then he loves a lame dog. Every year he buys so many
tickets for the spastic raffle he wins the TV set and every
year he gives it to an old folks' home. He used to try taking
me along on his visits but I said it wasn't me at all and he
gave up. One—place—we went, there were these poor freaks
with—oh, you know—enormous heads and so on—and you
just feel: oh, put them out of their misery. Well, they
wouldn't have survived in nature, it's only modern medicine,
so modern medicine should be allowed to do away with
them. A committee of doctors and do-gooders, naturally,
to make sure there's no funny business and then—if I say
gas-chamber that makes it sound horrid—but I do mean
put to sleep. When Freddie gets all mealy-mouthed about
it, I say, look, darling, if one of our kids was dying and
they had a cure and you knew it had been discovered in the
Nazi laboratories, would you refuse to let them use it? I
certainly wouldn't. I love my own immediate family and
that's the lot. Can't manage any more. I want to go home
and see them again. They may not be the most hard-
working, well-behaved geniuses on earth, but no one in
their right mind could say they were N.P.A. (*Turns back.*)
Freddie, I'm going. You can get a taxi and——
(SHEILA *carries* JOE *in, in her nightdress and dressing-gown.*)
SHEILA: Aaaah! The carols have stopped.
BRI: They've stopped, yes.
FREDDIE: This little Josephine?
SHEILA: This is Joe. Say hullo to Uncle Freddie.
FREDDIE (*shakes her hand*): Hullo, Joe, what do you know?
SHEILA: Not much, I'm afraid.
SHEILA: And Auntie Pamela.

PAM: She's got—really—a rather pretty face, hasn't she?

SHEILA: She's very P.L.U., when you get to know her. Aren't you, sweetheart?

BRI: I'm lovely, she says.

SHEILA: But strangely passive tonight. You didn't forget her medicine?

BRI: You'd be strangely passive, she says, if you'd been fitting and crying and doing doots.

SHEILA: But her eyes are hardly open.

BRI: Who wants to open their eyes in the middle of the night, she says. And one hour before midnight's worth two after, she says.

(*He embraces them both. He and* SHEILA *stand rocking* JOE.)

SHEILA: You missed the carol-singers, darling. What a shame.

BRI: Christmas already, she says. Seems to come round quicker every year.

SHEILA (*singing*): Away in a manger, no crib for a bed——
(BRI *joins her and they sing together, dancing her about the stage.*)
The little Lord Jesus laid down his head.
The stars in the bright sky looked down where He lay,
The little Lord Jesus asleep in the hay.

The cattle are lowing——
(*Near the end of the second verse* BRI *has to prevent her pushing away.*)

BRI: Oops!

SHEILA (*seeing at once*): Down here!
(*They put her in a chair facing upstage.*)

FREDDIE: What is it?

SHEILA: A fit. I thought she was too far gone for that——

FREDDIE: Nothing we can do?

BRI (*To* JOE): One day when you're doing that the wind will change and you'll stay like it.

SHEILA: D'you think she needs the doctor?

BRI: She should be in bed. I'll take her up.

SHEILA: What good's that? She's nearly unconscious.

BRI: What good's she doing down here?

(*Bell rings, front door.*)
That's the waits. I'll say we're Muslims.

SHEILA: Give them a shilling for Joe. I love the old customs, she says.

FREDDIE: Here—(*gives* BRI *money*)—from Joe.
(BRI *takes it awkwardly and goes off.*)

PAM: We must be off.

FREDDIE: I'd no idea she was so—torpid. One thinks of a Mongol or an athetoid or monoplegic. But—well—she really is *so* helpless.

SHEILA: She's worse than usual, aren't you, blossom?
(BRI *comes back.*)

BRI: It's my mother.
(*Makes frantic and spastic gestures and faces* SHEILA, *who silently appeals to the ceiling. They recover as* GRACE *follows in.*)

SHEILA: Hullo. How nice to see you!

GRACE: I'm not stopping, Sheila—oh. You didn't say you had company.

BRI: Mr. and Mrs. Underwood. My mother.

PAM: We were just going.

FREDDIE: How d'you do?

GRACE: No, I'm not stopping. Only I've been in town and thought I'd drop in Josephine's new cardie . . .
(*Comes to audience and speaks.* BRI *has taken her coat and goes off with it to the hall. Others light cigarettes, chat, etc., during her solo.* BRI *comes back and joins them.*)
(GRACE *is sixty-five, suburban, fastidious. Wears light-coloured suit with frilled decorations; gloves and shoes match handbag. Very short-sighted but refuses to wear spectacles. As well as her bag, she brings a hold-all full of shopping. Her manner is generally bright but gives way to spells of gloom when she tends to sigh a lot. In her presence,* BRI *is more boyish and struggles to escape her maternal allure.*)

GRACE: No, well I wouldn't have dropped in, not in the ordinary way, especially when they had company, only on Tuesday Mrs. Parry and I make a habit of meeting for the pictures if there's anything nice. Well, after you've been round with a

65

duster, there's nothing much to fill in the afternoons and no one wants to sit about like a mutt and don't laugh, will you, but they reduce the prices for old-age pensioners. I don't know whether anyone sees themself as an old-age pensioner —I know I don't, but when you're trying to manage on so little, a few shillings is a consideration. Not that my husband ever thought I'd be hard up—he paid enough for his private pension and his insurance in case something happened to him first—but there, they *say* it's the middle classes that have suffered the most, don't they, from inflation?

Anyway last week Mrs. Parry rang and said she couldn't see me Tuesday—that was on the Thursday—or was it Friday? —as she had to stay in for a vacuum. I said, "But surely to goodness a vacuum can come in the morning or any other afternoon, it doesn't have to be the very day we go out." She said, "My dear, nowadays if you're told to expect a vacuum Tuesday there's very little you can say to stop it." So I said, "Well, all right, I'll do some last-minute Christmas shopping in the afternoon and meet you in the Odeon café— what—about half past four?—and we can see Julie Andrews in the evening." Then—over the week-end I finished the cardigan I'd been knitting Josephine. Well—knitting passes the time and if you didn't have some diversion, you'd sit around like a blooming nun. No company, no one to talk to or have a cup of tea with. (*Sighs, wipes her nose and dabs the corners of her mouth.*)

I don't encourage neighbours. One thing can so easily lead to another with neighbours, you find them taking advantage. So it *is* very lonely, hour after hour, stuck like Joe Egg with no one to talk to. Why I do so many cardigans, the poor mite dribbles. Not in the way a baby dribbles even, worse than that. It's not nice to talk about, I know, but she can't seem to regulate the flow. Her garments, after a few hours on, they're stiff with saliva. (*Dabs corners of her mouth.*) Which means a lot of washing for her mother and I've said to Sheila often enough, "She should wear a plastic bib, it would be such a saving on wool," but of course you can't say a lot, can you, that's being an interfering mother-in-law. I do believe if I said, "Sheila, whatever you do, don't dress her in plastic bibs," that poor mite would be stuck in a plastic bib morning, noon and night like a blooming nun. (*Moves back to the others.*) And when we came out of the Odeon, I thought I'll go so far on Mrs. Parry's bus and drop in with my grand-daughter's cardigan and p'raps if Brian's not too busy he could run me home.

BRI: Yes, right.

GRACE: So I'm not stopping. (*Sits by* JOE.) And how's Nana's favourite girl tonight? Look what Nana's brought her. I'm fast asleep, she says.

SHEILA: She's poorly, very poorly.

GRACE: Having forty winks, she says.

BRI: She's all right.

GRACE: An hour before midnight's worth two after.

BRI: That's what they say.

GRACE: Let's see how it fits, shall we? (*While speaking, holds cardigan against* JOE.) Wouldn't she be lovely if she was running about?

FREDDIE: A beautiful child.

GRACE: First time you've seen her?

SHEILA: Why I brought her down.

GRACE: D'you think the sleeves are short, Sheila?

SHEILA: Her arms are so bent.

GRACE: You must allow for that, yes.

SHEILA: Yes.

GRACE: I fancy—a half-inch longer.

SHEILA: Would you bother?

GRACE: No bother. Got to do what little we can, haven't we?

FREDDIE: Yes, exactly.

GRACE (*still trying cardie*): You should have seen the shops this afternoon. I said to the lady in Scotch Wool and Hosiery, "You'll be glad when Christmas is over?"

BRI: What did she say to that?

GRACE: She said, "I certainly shall."

(BRI *shakes his head slowly in amazement.*)

But apart from the rush, I said to Mrs. Parry, it does look nice—the decorations and the toys and birds and toilet sets.

67

BRI: See Jesus?

GRACE: Pardon?

BRI: Did you see Jesus?

GRACE (*cautious, not looking at him*): Well, if I *did* I didn't notice.

BRI: On the electricity building.

GRACE (*tut-tutting*): They'll drag religion into anything. (*Pause. Looking at cardie.*) Colour's nice, isn't it? I think that sort of thing spoils Christmas.

BRI: Jesus?

GRACE (*making herself clear*): I think it's a time for children. Brian, d'you remember the very first year I took you to see Father Christmas?

BRI: Um——

GRACE: I shall never forget it. He took one look at him and said, "Mummy, I don't like that funny man."
(FREDDIE *laughs politely.* BRI *might not have heard.*)
But you loved the toy department. You used to say, "Oh, Mummy, I want it all, can I have it, Mummy, all to myself?"
(SHEILA *laughs uncontrollably.*)

BRI: We took Joe to Father Christmas. He stank of meths and he was handing out foam-rubber pandas and goosing the little girls——

FREDDIE: Why do you say these things?

BRI: It's true!

FREDDIE: It is *not* true. They're vetted.

BRI: We've got one! It stays in any position.

FREDDIE: Not the pandas. The—other——

BRI: That was true. Soon as Joe sat on his lap, she had a fit. That stopped him.

GRACE (*she scratches, to* SHEILA): D'you know, I believe I've acquired a little visitor? Not what you expect from the Odeon.

BRI: You got it here. Off our cat. We're infested with them.

GRACE: Are you really, Sheila? Fleas is something I don't believe we've ever had. Can you remember, Brian?

BRI: An occasional wood-louse.

GRACE: Not the same as fleas. (*She moves about nervously.*)

SHEILA: It's Beatrice Webb. We keep her outside now.

68

GRACE: I should. I know you're very fond of animals, Sheila, but surely it's an interest you must keep in proportion.

SHEILA. It's the first time we've ever had them.

GRACE: They say there's a first time for everything, don't they? (*Sits by* JOE *again.*) Don't they, loveliest girl in all the wide wide world.

SHEILA: Look! Another fit.

(GRACE *stands and moves backwards.*)

GRACE: Bless her heart!

(SHEILA *examines* JOE.)

SHEILA: She's worse. Look at this.

BRI: She's sleeping it off. (*And to* GRACE.) They left off her medicine at the centre and now——

SHEILA: How can you say that?

BRI: What?

SHEILA: Sleeping it off.

GRACE: I should have it destroyed.

SHEILA: Another dose of medicine. (*Goes to kitchen.*)

GRACE: If it was me.

BRI: What, Mum?

GRACE: I should have whatever-you-call-her put to sleep.

(BRI *looks at her, having only heard this.*)

FREDDIE: The cat.

BRI: Oh.

GRACE: Fleas bring disease.

(BRI *sits by* JOE *and examines her intently, looking to kitchen anxiously.*)

PAM: In my daughter's primary school, they had a plague of bugs brought in by some poor council-house kiddies——

FREDDIE: How d'you *know* it was them?

PAM (*frightened of his anger*): 'Twasn't the *kiddies'* fault.

GRACE: I blame the parents.

PAM: Emma got the most hideous rash.

GRACE: Some children are more susceptible, more sensitive. Brian always had a delicate skin.

BRI: All right, Mum.

GRACE: Look at his impetigo.

(SHEILA *comes from kitchen with empty bottle.*)

69

SHEILA: I can only find this empty one. Where's it all gone?

BRI: Oh yeah! She spilt it. Joe. Knocked it over. (*Pause.*)
Having a fit. I had to save her first.

SHEILA: But it's like treacle. How did it get poured out?

BRI: Well, it did.

SHEILA: It's been washed clean.

BRI: I saved enough to give her a dose, then washed it out.
(*Pause. She puts bottle down.*)

SHEILA: You must get some more.

BRI: She's had enough sedation for one night.
(*They all look at her.*)
I'm turned on, she says.

SHEILA: She's having fits.

BRI: Not bad ones.

SHEILA: They weaken her. She needs the anti-convulsant.

BRI: But what time is it?

PAM: Twenty to eleven.

BRI: There you are!

GRACE: Boots is open. On the Centre.

FREDDIE: Shall I go?

BRI: No, I'll manage.

SHEILA: Here's the prescription.

GRACE: I should wrap up warm, Brian. Put a scarf on.
(*She speaks to* PAM, *with whom she senses an affinity.*)
He's always been a martyr to colds. I've known him come in
crying with his poor little fingers all yellow and all the other
boys still out running about and I've had to rub them and
get him a warm drink and sit him by the fire till he was over
it . . .
(BRI *listens to this, then smiles at them all and goes.*)

SHEILA (*holding* JOE's *hand*): What's funny daddy been up to, eh,
my rose?
(*Pause.* FREDDIE's *attention drawn.*)

FREDDIE: You think he's up to something?

SHEILA: That medicine's thick. You couldn't spill much. The
bottle was full, I don't know. He *told* us he'd killed her.

FREDDIE: That wasn't true, so we needn't——

GRACE: Told you what?

70

SHEILA: He'd killed her. Yes.

GRACE: Oh, no.

FREDDIE: It was an adolescent joke.

GRACE: His jokes, I never listen.

FREDDIE: Showing off to get attention.

GRACE: It *is* showing off.

SHEILA: Like a baby. By saying that he could take my attention off poor Joe and get it on himself again. And when that palled, he'd make up another—with himself as the killer or the corpse or—anything—as long as it's the most important part.

GRACE: I can't imagine Brian doing that without provocation.

FREDDIE: Oh, no. The other joke we've had this evening was that Sheila and I are having a love affair. And for that, I assure you, we neither of us gave him the slightest provocation.

GRACE: Perhaps not *you*. I couldn't say.

SHEILA: Hullo?

GRACE: But I shouldn't wonder if Brian thought there was something—going on——

FREDDIE: Why?

GRACE: Perhaps—knowing what he did—he was apt to be over-suspicious——

SHEILA: Knowing what he——

GRACE: Probably expected it. (*To* PAM.) I mean always. Half expected it.

SHEILA: What d'you mean.

GRACE: No. Nothing.

SHEILA: Come on.

FREDDIE: Frankly I resent the——

GRACE: I didn't mean to say that, no——

SHEILA: Why should he have expected it?

GRACE: Don't you know?

SHEILA: No.

GRACE: I think you do, Sheila. Brian knew all about your past life even before he married you.

SHEILA: Of course he did. *I* told him.

GRACE: Yes.

SHEILA: How do *you* know about it?

71

GRACE: He told me.

SHEILA: Ah!

FREDDIE: Lord above!

PAM: This is horrid!

FREDDIE: Have you heard the car start?

SHEILA: I'd love to have heard what you said when he told you.

PAM: I haven't, no.

GRACE: I'll tell you.

FREDDIE: I'll go and see.

GRACE: I said, "You must make up your own mind, Brian."

FREDDIE (*to* SHEILA): Going to help Brian. (*Exit to front door.*)

SHEILA: Bet you had a shock when he did.

GRACE: Meaning what exactly?

SHEILA: Meaning you always made his mind up for him.

GRACE (*to* PAM): *This* is nice.

SHEILA: You spoilt him.

GRACE: I must say!

SHEILA: Wrecked him.

GRACE: Thank you.

> (*Silence. Both women momentarily spent. They move about.*)

SHEILA: Where's Freddie?

PAM: The car hadn't started. He's gone to help.

SHEILA: Not started——

> (*Makes to go out but* BRI *and* FREDDIE *come in.*)

BRI: Can't get it started.

FREDDIE: Have you tried, I wonder? You were sitting in it doing
   nothing when I——

PAM: Let me go. In my car.

SHEILA: Would you?

PAM: I should have gone before. (*Aside.*) Anything to get away.

BRI: Shall I come—show you a short cut.

PAM: No need.

> (*She is going.*)

FREDDIE: Got the chitty?

PAM: What?

FREDDIE (*to* BRI): Give her the prescription.

> (BRI *finds it, gives it to her, dropping it, picking it up, etc.*)

SHEILA: It's yellow, looks like custard.

(PAM *goes*.)

BRI: Twenty-five quid that car cost me and after only three years look at it!

GRACE: You were never very clever with your hands. You took after your father there. (*To* FREDDIE.) Poor old thing used to spend hours on end behind the radiogram and in the end we'd have to call the proper man.

SHEILA (*suddenly, vehemently, to* BRI): Great spoilt baby! Coddled baby!

FREDDIE: Now, Sheila, there's no use——

SHEILA (*to* FREDDIE): The only way he knows to get what he wants is screaming and stamping his feet, but that's a bit grotesque at his age, so he straightaway says Poor Me, but nobody listens so he makes some jokes and everybody laughs, which is better than nothing, so he makes more and more jokes and when everyone else has gone I get the "poor me", I have to swallow that. (*Turns on* GRACE.) Because you *spoilt* him.

FREDDIE: Now, Sheila, we've had our——

GRACE: I kept the house free of fleas, I admit that. I spring-cleaned every year instead of once in five. Certainly when he was a tiny mite I used to press his ears back for fear they'd protrude. I boiled a kettle in his room for croup. Made a mustard bath for the cold and kept out the wind. I believe in an insulated house. (*To* BRI.) It's still insulated, Brian, it's still home. You're welcome, I've told you that. 'Specially since I was left alone. Not so much a home these days as a blooming nunnery. I'm stuck up there day after day like a blooming nun.

SHEILA (*to* FREDDIE): There you are. "Poor me!"

FREDDIE: Sssh!

GRACE: What did you say?

SHEILA: Your self-pity. Just like him. Poor me!

GRACE: Wait till *you're* alone.

SHEILA: Why don't you move in with your friend?

GRACE: Mrs. Parry?

SHEILA: Yes. Why not? There you sit in your perfectly insulated houses each with your own TV and stove and lawn-mower and empty garage, each complaining continually about being

73

a blooming nun. What's stopping you?

GRACE: You want your privacy.

SHEILA: Do you? I don't. I hate it.

GRACE: Wouldn't do if we were all alike.

SHEILA (*suddenly to* FREDDIE): You see their selfishness! We're talking about them again, d'you notice? Here's Joe—I think she's seriously ill—and—what are we doing?
(*Noticing* JOE *again, she stops, goes down by her, looks at her closely.*)

GRACE: Has the poor mite ever been anything *but* seriously ill?

SHEILA: We must call the doctor. She's white as chalk but her lips are blue. Straining the heart, you see.

BRI: I'll take her back to bed, let her sleep it off.

SHEILA: Her chest is hardly moving.

BRI: A touch of flatulence, she says.

SHEILA · No.

BRI: Heartburn.
(SHEILA *stares at him. He goes to pick up* JOE.)

SHEILA: Leave her!
(BRI *leaves her.*)

GRACE: She ought to be in hospital.

SHEILA: I'll go if nobody else will.

GRACE: Ought to have gone in years ago.

SHEILA: But don't let Brian touch her.

GRACE: Then the marriage would have had a chance.
(SHEILA *refuses to rise, makes to go to door.*)
You can't expect a man to take second place to a child like that.

FREDDIE: Now, now.

GRACE: It's not *his* fault she's spastic!

SHEILA: What was that? Not *his* fault? Whose then?

GRACE: No one's.

SHEILA: Come on.

GRACE: I didn't mean that. Not your fault either. You can't help the family you were born into. When it's congenital it's not your fault, no——

SHEILA (*to* FREDDIE): What's she talking about?

GRACE: Fits I'm talking about.

74

(*Pause.*)

SHEILA: What?

GRACE: Your uncle's fits.

SHEILA: Uncle's fits—which uncle?

GRACE: Which one was it, Brian?

SHEILA: You told her my uncle had fits?

BRI: Oh, Mum!

GRACE: You did.

BRI (*to* SHEILA): Your cousin Geoff.

SHEILA: Infant convulsions. What baby doesn't have infant convulsions?

GRACE: Well, none of the babies in *our* family, for a start!

SHEILA: I take that for granted, dear. (*To* BRI.) What made you mention cousin Geoff to her like that? You know she'd——

BRI (*nodding, pacifying*): She'd just been telling *me* about the epilepsy in our family.

GRACE: I beg your pardon?

BRI: And I felt I had to console her by mentioning someone on your side. You pick your time to throw it back, don't you?

GRACE: Epilepsy in our family? Where d'you get that?

BRI: From you! Uncle Neville.

GRACE: Uncle Neville! Oh! (*Laughs.*)

BRI: Yes, Uncle Neville.

GRACE: He wasn't family. He happened to marry Auntie May, that's all.

BRI: So our family's only epileptic by marriage!

GRACE (*agreeing readily*): Of course! But I will say this for May. She didn't have children. Mrs. Parry said to me, "I think if you know there's a taint in the family you should refrain from children."

SHEILA: She'd welcome any excuse—that walking sheath.

GRACE: Please don't use language to me. Brian, you stand about like a mutt while she picks on your mother in company.

BRI: Not you, Mum—Mrs. Parry.

GRACE: My best friend.

BRI: You don't expect me to defend Mrs. Parry. (*Mad Doctor*) Nurse, Nurse, we've done it, I tell you! With this we can make whole continents barren. The deterrent they've all been working for—Mrs. Parry! (*Mad laugh.*)

(*Silence.*)

GRACE: I thought you were serious for a moment.

BRI: Come on. I'll take you home.

GRACE (*startled*): What? Back to the nunnery.

BRI: That's right, yes.

GRACE: Thank you. That's gratitude. (*She is tearful now that he shows which side he's on.*)

FREDDIE: Thought you couldn't start the car.

BRI: No, but if I crank it——

FREDDIE: You mean you didn't crank it before——

(FREDDIE *and* SHEILA *look at each other.*)

GRACE: I had a tartan grip.

SHEILA: What about Joe? You leaving Freddie alone with her?

BRI: Why? You going somewhere?

SHEILA: To phone the doctor.

BRI: I'll do that when I get back. If you really want to bother him.

SHEILA: No, we'll do it now. She's unconscious.

BRI: I'll only *be* twenty minutes.

SHEILA: Half an hour, if we're *lucky*. She'll make tea.

BRI: I shan't stop for tea.

GRACE: I've got some Garibaldis, I know you——

BRI: Right, I'll ring from there. (*To* GRACE.) Can I do that?

GRACE: Have I ever said no to you?

BRI (*to* SHEILA): All right?

SHEILA: No. Do it now.

FREDDIE: *I'll* do it.

BRI: Eh?

FREDDIE: While you're taking your mother home. From a local phone-box.

SHEILA: Would you, Freddie?

FREDDIE: Sure!

BRI: You interfering bastard!

FREDDIE: I'm trying to help you——

BRI: Help? You're a pain in the arse.

GRACE (*aside*): I hate a play with language.

SHEILA: Have you got a threepenny-piece?

(FREDDIE *searches in his pockets for money while they talk.*)

GRACE: I might have one in my bag.
  (*She searches too.*)
FREDDIE: What you're suggesting is no way out.
BRI: There's no other possible way——
FREDDIE: Once start that—we'll have anarchy.
BRI: That'd be something.
FRDDIE: Don't be childish, you must have order. "Thou shalt not kill."
BRI: Except when it shall come to pass that thy trade-routes shall be endangered.
GRACE: I could have sworn I had a threepenny-piece.
BRI: Then shalt thou slay as many as possible of the enemies of General Motors and I.C.I.
SHEILA: How about you, Freddie?
FREDDIE: Nothing but half-crowns and pennies.
SHEILA: My bag's upstairs.
FREDDIE: Suppose euthanasia was legalized and your daughter let die. Then twenty years from now a cure is found.
SHEILA: Any luck?
GRACE: Pennies and shillings. What's this—I can't see.
SHEILA: A milk check.
FREDDIE: Just imagine.
BRI: You mean her brain starts working?
SHEILA: Give me a shilling.
BRI: A six-weeks-old brain in a thirty-years-old body.
SHEILA: No, that's a halfpenny.
GRACE: This light's so dim. And these nasty creatures itching.
FREDDIE: No, some kind of grafting.
BRI: An adult brain?
FREDDIE: I don't know. Yes!
SHEILA: Brian, have you got a threepenny-piece?
  (BRI *starts looking.*)
BRI: Say, the brain of a woman who died at thirty? Here's one.
  (SHEILA *takes it.*)
  Whose soul will she have?
SHEILA: Here, Freddie.
  (*Gives him coin.*)
BRI: I think that question should go to our popular TV mini-

bishop. Your Grace—hey—just a minute!

(*Grabs back coin. They struggle.*)

FREDDIE: What are we doing? I'll dial emergency. The hospital.

SHEILA: Yes, the ambulance! Say it's urgent. I'll show you the box.

GRACE: Put a coat on, though. It's bitter.

(*But they've gone.*)

And you wrap yourself up properly too, Brian, if you're running me home.

(*She takes from her handbag cosmetic articles and spends the next few minutes doing her face, hardly aware of what is happening behind her.*)

Going out of the warm on a night like this is the best way if you want to catch cold. We came out of the Odeon and it was cutting down Union Street like a knife.

(BRI, *hardly listening, goes to* JOE *and listens for her heart, feels her pulse.*)

I said to Mrs. Parry, "Oh, my Lord, what a night!" She said they said we were in for something of the sort possibly lasting into February. I said, "It's a shame for the old people" and she said, "Grace, I hate to remind you but we're the old people now." I said, "Well, if I've got to stand about waiting for buses in this, I shall catch my death."

(BRI *looks up.* GRACE *goes on making up.* BRI *looks at* JOE, *then towards front door. He lifts the child and throws her over one shoulder. He goes out the kitchen door with her, closing it behind him.*)

I said, "I may be old but I'm not quite ready to go yet." So if you're running me, I should put on something warm because it's not so much the cold as the contrast.

(*Looks round, sees he has gone, continues to audience.*)

Talking to myself. No, but it's an old car with no heater and draughts from all directions and he's always been susceptible to cold.

(SHEILA *comes back from front door into room.*)

Well, if it's in your nature, I say it's nothing to be ashamed of.

SHEILA: Where's Joe?

GRACE: Pardon?

SHEILA: Joe's gone.

GRACE: How can she have gone?

(*Sees she has.*)

SHEILA: He's taken her. Where?

GRACE: He didn't say.

(*During this,* BRI *carries* JOE *across behind* SHEILA *from back door of house to front door.*)

SHEILA (*angry*): Didn't you see him go?

GRACE: One minute I was talking to him, next I was talking to myself.

(SHEILA *turns and goes to bottom of stairs, calls.*)

SHEILA: Bri!

(*She runs off upstairs.*)

GRACE: I expect he's put her to bed, poor mite. She shouldn't be sitting up here all hours, I thought that when I came in.

(*Talks to audience again.*)

Brian's Dad used to say—when he was getting on— "Grace, I've had my life, if only I could give her what's left to me, I would." I believe he meant it too. Though, of course, as it turned out, there wasn't much left to him because he died the following year.

(*Hear* SHEILA *call* BRI *upstairs, as* BRI *enters from front door.*)

BRI: You ready, Mum?

GRACE: What?

BRI: Ready to go, are you?

GRACE: I'm getting ready.

BRI: Put your coat on then.

GRACE: Aren't you going to put one on?

BRI: No time. I'll try and get the engine started.

GRACE: You know what that engine's like. Get that started first.

(SHEILA *comes downstairs.* GRACE *suddenly remembers and asks:*)

What have you done with Josephine?

SHEILA: Bri!

(BRI *runs off to kitchen, closing door.* SHEILA *comes into room.*)

SHEILA: He's not up there. Not anywhere. He must have gone outside.

GRACE: He's just been here.

SHEILA: With Joe?

GRACE: No.

SHEILA: Where's he gone?

GRACE: Out there.

SHEILA: The garden?——

(SHEILA *goes out to kitchen, leaving door.*)

GRACE: Oh, mind the cats.

(*Shuts kitchen door and scratches.* BRI *enters at main door with* GRACE'S *overcoat.*)

BRI: Ready, Mum?

GRACE: What on earth's the rush? Have you got the car running?

BRI: Let's get inside first. I can push it if it won't go.

GRACE: Mind you don't strain yourself.

BRI: Put your coat on.

GRACE: Sheila's just gone off to the garden after you.

BRI: Get a move on.

GRACE: What have you done with the baby?

BRI: Me? Nothing. Hasn't Sheila got her?

GRACE: Sheila's *look*ing for her.

(*He has now got* GRACE'S *coat on.*)

GRACE: I've got to talk to Sheila about the cardigan.

BRI: Not now, Mum.

(*He collects her stuff and is about to go.*)

Come on!

GRACE: Aren't you waiting for your friend to come? Here's Sheila now——

(*And* BRI *runs off by main door with* GRACE'S *carrier.* SHEILA *comes from garden through kitchen.*)

SHEILA: No sign of them. And it's snowing now.

GRACE: Snowing? My Lord! Brian, I should put something on——

(*Sees he has gone.*)

SHEILA: Was he here?

GRACE: Where's he gone now?

SHEILA: With Joe.

GRACE: Must have gone to the car.

80

SHEILA: Did he have Joe with him?

GRACE: No. He hadn't seen her. He was rushing me off my feet, but I said, "I must ask Sheila whether she wants anything else done to Josephine's cardigan—apart from the sleeves——"

(SHEILA *has gone to look in the hall. Now there is an explosion in the kitchen—not very loud but loud enough to stop* GRACE *speaking and cause* SHEILA *to come back into room. It is followed by the sounds of glass or crockery falling.*)

My Lord——

SHEILA: There he is!

GRACE: Sounded more like the gas. D'you leave the gas on?

(SHEILA *goes out to kitchen.*)

Mind don't let the cats in.

SHEILA (*off*): All this glass and stick!

GRACE: What is it?

(*She goes off, shutting door.*)

(FREDDIE *and* PAM *come in from front,* PAM *carrying bottle of yellow medicine.*)

FREDDIE: Must be upstairs.

PAM: But why the front door open?

(SHEILA *comes on from kitchen.*)

FREDDIE: Ah! They're sending an ambulance.

PAM: The front door's open.

FREDDIE: I met Pam coming in.

GRACE: What a mess!

FREDDIE: What?

GRACE: Glass and sticky stuff.

SHEILA: The ginger-beer plant exploded.

GRACE: I thought it sounded more like the gas.

SHEILA: Brian must have put a screwtop on. I've told him to use a cork. It gives when the pressure builds up inside.

GRACE: Nuisance—anything like that with a life of its own.

FREDDIE: Where *is* Brian?

SHEILA: He's gone mad. He's running about outside. With Joe.

FREDDIE: Outside?

PAM: D'you know it's snowing again?

FREDDIE: We didn't see him.

81

PAM: The door was open.

SHEILA: Snowing——

(*Makes towards front door but* BRI *comes in carrying* JOE.)

BRI: I think it's all over.

(*Puts her on sofa.*)

FREDDIE: What's all over?

BRI: You look at her.

(SHEILA *kneels by sofa, takes* JOE *in her arms, nurses and warms her, wrapping her about, rocking her.*)

SHEILA: My poor blossom——

FREDDIE (*quiet, authoritative*): What happened?

BRI: I took her outside.

FREDDIE: And did what?

BRI: Nothing. Left her lying on the back seat of the car.

FREDDIE: What for?

SHEILA: —little worm, poor little worm——

BRI: Something Mum said suggested it——

GRACE: Me? I never suggested taking——

BRI: No.

GRACE: On a night like this?

BRI: But you said——

GRACE: Is it likely?

BRI: You said it was bitter cold. I was going to leave her in the garden but I couldn't——

SHEILA: Can anyone do the kiss of life?

FREDDIE: I can't. *He feels his inadequacy*

BRI: So in the end I put her in the car. I don't know what I wanted—just to stop them saving her again. When you went to phone I thought——

FREDDIE (*to* SHEILA): Can you feel a pulse?

SHEILA: No. I can't. Oh, my poor dove. She's freezing.

FREDDIE: The shock might have done it.

GRACE: Oh, my Lord. Brian, whatever made you do a thing like that——

(GRACE *takes one of* JOE's *hands and rubs it vigorously between hers.*)

FREDDIE: Have you got a looking-glass?

GRACE: One in my handbag——

82

SHEILA: Come along, my bird, my little dove——
> (FREDDIE *searches in* GRACE's *bag.*)
GRACE: Oh, Brian, you shouldn't, not however bad she was, poor
little mite, you shouldn't deliberately do that.
FREDDIE: Here's a glass.
> (*Wipes it, gives it to* SHEILA, *who holds it by* JOE's *mouth.*)
SHEILA: Sweetheart, come on, sweetheart, try for Mummy——
> (BRI *watches in dismay. The others are grouped round the sofa.*)
—come on, dearest love, gonna be all right now . . .
> (BRI *moves away, sits on his own.*)
GRACE: Perhaps the glass isn't cold enough. To get the condensa-
tion. A piece of fluff——
PAM: What?
GRACE: A feather will show the slightest draught.
> (*She searches in cushions for a feather.*)
PAM (*to* FREDDIE): This is ghastly.
GRACE: Is this a feather?
FREDDIE: Yes.
GRACE: There. Close to her mouth. This is how we knew poor Dad
had gone.
> (*Front doorbell.*)
FREDDIE: Here they are. Don't say anything, anyone. I'll answer
the questions. You concentrate on the child. No need for
unnecessary suffering. All right?——
SHEILA: Sweet flower, come along now——
> (*They lift her and move in a group toward the door.*)
GRACE (*to* PAM): Wouldn't she have been lovely if she'd been
running about?
> (*Fade lights.*)
> (BRI *comes down to forestage.*)
BRI: Sheila and I went with her in the ambulance. Mum stayed in
Pam's car waiting for news. It was all-stations go in the
hospital—voluntary women rushing everywhere with soup
and Bibles . . . St. Bernards standing by . . .
> (*Mimes hand-mike, assumes awe-stricken voice.*)
If there *is* anything heartening about such a disaster, I think
it's the wonderful way this great operation of mercy has
moved into action. And of course the uniquely British

optimism that suddenly in moments of crisis seems to suffuse
the whole nauseating atmosphere. I remember—when they
first came in, the husband was jibbering and shaking like
some spineless dago but nobody quite knew what to do.
Then one of the impressive Lesbian nurses pointed to the
African orderlies and said quietly, "Pull yourself together,
man, set an example . . ."
(*Drops the parody.*)
Anyway the sawbones got to work with the oil-can and . . .
"I think there's a chance, Nurse . . . all our work may not be
wasted."
And the upshot was—finally Mum's feather fluttered.
(*He looks at the set, pausing for some seconds.*)
Sheila could hardly stand, what with anxiety and relief, so
they gave her a bed for the night. Joe was staying in, of course,
they couldn't say how long but perhaps a week.
I went in Freddie's car when he ran my mother back to the
nunnery. She begged me to stay with her. "I'll fill a nice
hot-water bottle," she said. And when I stood my ground,
"How about my electric blanket?" And I said, "No, Mum.
Cheerio, I'll be in touch," and she started on about lighting
the Valor stove that I loved so much because it threw patterns
of light on the bedroom ceiling. I nearly choked with longing
for that, but I gritted my teeth and said no, there was the
budgie to be fed. And she said she had my old dummy and
rattle somewhere . . . so in the end I ran . . . Freddie was a
hoot. Saying it was a lucky escape and a blessing and stuff
like that. His trouble, he's too kind-hearted, too squeamish.
And he clings to law and order. Pam now. She's got the
right idea. For the wrong reasons. Or something.
Look at me, delivering judgment. Who do you think you are
—God? So—after they'd dropped me home—off they went
to their three absolutely gorgeous kiddies—everyone a
company director—and the oil-fired heating—the labour-
saving evergreens . . . the fibre-glass yacht. I was glad to see
the back of him. You can't think with that loud-hailer going
on and on. Not that there was *much* to think about. Only
details.

Our marriage might have worked as well as most if Joe hadn't happened. I was too young for it, that's true, of course. I always will be. But Sheila might just have dragged me screaming into manhood. 'Stead of which, I was one of the menagerie. She loved me as much as any goldfish or aphelandra. So now it was a question of how to tell her I was leaving her. And when I went into it, I saw it wouldn't only be about Joe, but also my ambitions . . . and the first time I saw Father Christmas and—this backache's worse than yesterday and—the pattern on the ceiling . . . so in the end I better just creep away without a word . . .

(*Goes into room and begins hurriedly putting various objects into his pockets, putting on coat, etc.*)

So I've shaved and washed and packed a case . . .

(*Gets case from hall, stands it near by.*)

haven't decided where I'm going yet. Up the smoke, I suppose, get lost among the Australians.

(*Looks at watch.*)

Ordinary way I'd be leaving now for eyes-front-hands-on-heads . . . but never again, I tell you! Want a nice slow job . . . game-warden . . . keeper at Regent's Park . . . better still Kew Gardens . . .

(*Looks at room, his back to us, fixing it for ever.*)

Well.

Noise off; BRI *dodges behind wall. He looks for a way out but* SHEILA *enters. She doesn't see him, he attempts to go out and she hears him. He draws guns and fires on her.*)

SHEILA: You're up. I thought you'd lie in.

BRI: I've got school.

SHEILA: You're not going?

BRI: Yes.

SHEILA: No. Go absent.

BRI: Only two more days. How are you?

(*But* SHEILA *looks towards the front door again.*)

SHEILA (*calling*): Thank you.

(*She goes to front door.* BRI *looks for escape routes—other door, window, etc., but despairs.* SHEILA *comes back wheeling* JOE *in her chair.*)

85

SHEILA: There we are, lovely. Home again.

(*She leaves her centre.* BRI *goes to them.*)

BRI: I thought they were keeping her in for a few days.

SHEILA: They wanted to but—really—what's the point? I've
nursed her through pneumonia, 'flu, more colds than I can
count. Why bother busy nurses?

(*They stand or crouch either side of* JOE *as at her first
appearance.*)

Anyway, Dad, did you *see* the nurses? And the doctors?

BRI: How d'you mean, Mum?

SHEILA: Every one a fuzzy-wuzzy.

BRI: I thought it was alright *doctors* being black.

SHEILA: She didn't fancy it, Dad.

BRI: How are you, lovely?

SHEILA: Still a bit dopey but her pulse is stronger and she's
breathing well. She's as tough as old boots, Dad. She'll get
the Queen's Telegram yet, you see.

(BRI *smiles.* JOE *sighs and turns her head. They look at her.
That's all.* BRI *stands. Looks at his watch.*)

SHEILA: But she's certainly not well enough for school. Not this
term. And you're not *going* either.

BRI: Yes, I must, love——

(SHEILA *moves to him.*)

SHEILA: All night I've being saying to myself we'll spend a few
days in bed together. Come on . . .

(*Starts unbuttoning his coat.*)

I'll ring the Head if you're frightened.

BRI: Not fair on the other staff.

(*He struggles and she tickles him. He giggles.*)

SHEILA: I thought, I'll get home before he's up and make him
bacon and eggs—and fried apple rings. Did you have
something hot?

BRI: Tea and toast, yes. And I've fed the zoo and tidied up.

SHEILA: And I'll take them up to him, I thought, and after that I'll
climb in with him. And look what I find. So I shall have to
get all those clothes off him and we'll stay all day with the
snow outside . . . cold and quiet . . . and us in there up to our
tricks.

(*She embraces him. He has left off struggling.*)

86

Last night I lay there thinking what you'd tried to do to
Joe——

BRI (*quickly*): I was round the twist—you know, my Mum,
Freddie——

SHEILA: No, I don't blame you, honestly. It was my fault. I've been
asking too much. But listen—d'you know what I'm going to
do? I'm going to look for a residential hospital where I'm
sure she'll be well looked after and won't pine. And when I've
found it, d'you know what?
(*She is facing down. He looks at her.*)
You and I will leave her there—for, I don't know—several
weeks, even a month, every year. Means we'll be able to go
abroad. Haven't been abroad for eleven years. Second
honeymoon, alright? And let's start now.
(*Her hands are all over him.*)

BRI: I'll go and ring the school.
(*He gets free.*)

SHEILA: Run all the way there and back. I can't wait long. And
even though you're only going a few yards, I should wrap up
warm. It's brilliant sun but treacherous underfoot.

BRI: I'll be in the car.

SHEILA: What, just to go round there?

BRI: Case it's occupied I can always try another.

SHEILA: Back in one piece then, and you will be quick? Mmm?

BRI: Right.
(*He stands looking at her. She is on her way to the kitchen, but
feels forced to say more.*)

SHEILA: I shall go on up. Will you carry Joe to her room when you
come up? She's such a lump.
(BRI *nods. She goes into the kitchen,* BRI *picks up his case and
goes. Door slams off.* SHEILA *comes back, closes door on cats,
scratches arm.*)
(*To fish.*) Daddy fed you? He is good.
(*To bird.*) Got some seed? What a daddy!
(*To* JOE.) Aren't we lucky?
(*She goes out and up the stairs.* JOE *remains.*)

CURTAIN

Selected Grove Press Theater Paperbacks

17061-X ARDEN, JOHN / Plays: One (Serjeant Musgrave's Dance; The Workhouse Donkey; Armstrong's Last Goodnight) / $4.95

17083-0 AYCKBOURN, ALAN / Absurd Person Singular, Absent Friends, Bedroom Farce: Three Plays / $6.95

17208-6 BECKETT, SAMUEL / Endgame / $3.95

17233-7 BECKETT, SAMUEL / Happy Days / $4.95

62061-5 BECKETT, SAMUEL / Ohio Impromptu, Catastrophe, and What Where: Three Plays / $4.95

17204-3 BECKETT, SAMUEL / Waiting for Godot / $4.95

13034-8 BRECHT, BERTOLT / Galileo / $4.95

17472-0 BRECHT, BERTOLT / The Threepenny Opera / $3.95

17411-9 CLURMAN, HAROLD / Nine Plays of the Modern Theater (Waiting for Godot by Samuel Beckett; The Visit by Friedrich Durrenmatt; Tango by Slawomir Mrozek; The Caucasian Chalk Circle by Bertolt Brecht; The Balcony by Jean Genet; Rhinoceros by Eugene Ionesco; American Buffalo by David Mamet; The Birthday Party by Harold Pinter; and Rosencrantz and Guildenstern Are Dead by Tom Stoppard) / $15.95

17535-2 COWARD, NOEL / Three Plays (Private Lives; Hay Fever; Blithe Spirit) / $7.95

17239-6 DURRENMATT, FRIEDRICH / The Visit / $5.95

17214-0 GENET, JEAN / The Balcony / $7.95

17390-2 GENET, JEAN / The Maids and Deathwatch: Two Plays / $8.95

7022-9 HAYMAN, RONALD / How to Read a Play / $6.95

7075-X INGE, WILLIAM / Four Plays (Come Back, Little Sheba; Picnic; Bus Stop; The Dark at the Top of the Stairs) / $8.95

62199-9 IONESCO, EUGENE / Exit the King, The Killer and Macbett / $9.95

7209-4 IONESCO, EUGENE / Four Plays (The Bald Soprano; The Lesson; The Chairs; Jack or The Submission) $6.95

7226-4 IONESCO, EUGENE / Rhinoceros and Other Plays (The Leader; The Future Is in Eggs; or It Takes All Sorts to Make a World) / $6.95

7485-2 JARRY, ALFRED / The Ubu Plays (Ubu Rex; Ubu Cuckolded; Ubu Enchained) / $9.95

7744-4 KAUFMAN, GEORGE and HART, MOSS / Three Plays (Once in a Lifetime; You Can't Take It With You; The Man Who Came to Dinner) / $8.95

17016-4 MAMET, DAVID / American Buffalo / $5.95
62049-6 MAMET, DAVID / Glengarry Glen Ross / $6.95
17040-7 MAMET, DAVID / A Life in the Theatre / $9.95
17043-1 MAMET, DAVID / Sexual Perversity in Chicago and The Duck Variations / $7.95
17264-7 MROZEK, SLAWOMIR / Tango / $3.95
17092-X ODETS, CLIFFORD / Six Plays (Waiting for Lefty; Awake and Sing; Golden Boy; Rocket to the Moon; Till the Day I Die; Paradise Lost) / $7.95
17001-6 ORTON, JOE / The Complete Plays (The Ruffian on the Stair; The Good and Faithful Servant; The Erpingham Camp; Funeral Games; Loot; What the Butler Saw; Entertaining Mr. Sloan) / $9.95
17084-9 PINTER, HAROLD / Betrayal / $6.95
17019-9 PINTER, HAROLD / Complete Works: One (The Birthday Party; The Room; The Dumb Waiter; A Slight Ache; A Night Out; The Black and White; The Examination) $8.95
17020-2 PINTER, HAROLD / Complete Works: Two (The Caretaker; Night School; The Dwarfs; The Collection; The Lover; Five Revue Sketches) / $6.95
17051-2 PINTER, HAROLD / Complete Works: Three (The Homecoming; Landscape; Silence; The Basement; Six Revue Sketches; Tea party [play]; Tea Party [short story]; Mac) / $6.95
17950-1 PINTER, HAROLD / Complete Works: Four (Old Times; No Man's Land; Betrayal; Monologue; Family Voices) / $5.95
17251-5 PINTER, HAROLD / The Homecoming / $5.95
17885-8 PINTER, HAROLD / No Man's Land / $7.95
17539-5 POMERANCE, BERNARD / The Elephant Man / $5.95
17743-6 RATTIGAN, TERENCE / Plays: One (French Without Tears; The Winslow Boy; Harlequinade; The Browning Version) / $5.95
62040-2 SETO, JUDITH ROBERTS / The Young Actor's Workbook / $8.95
17948-X SHAWN, WALLACE and GREGORY, ANDRÉ / My Dinner with André / $6.95
13033-X STOPPARD, TOM / Rosencrantz and Guildenstern Are Dead / $4.95
17884-X STOPPARD, TOM / Travesties / $4.95
17206-X WALEY, ARTHUR, tr. and ed. / The Nō Plays of Japan / $7.95

GROVE PRESS, 841 Broadway, New York, N.Y. 10003